THE SM
SUPPLY

A bold & revolutionary business approach to
create the smart **disruptive business.**

S. Shawn Paul &
Prof. Wilfred D. Paul

BlueRose
Publishers

First Published in July 2019

BLUEROSE PUBLISHERS
www.bluerosepublishers.com
info@bluerosepublishers.com
+91 8882 898 898

Cover Design:
Tyngshain Pariat

Typographic Design:
Teena Maurya

Editor:
Swati Malik

Distributed by: Blue Rose, Amazon, Flipkart, Shopclues

ACKNOWLEDGEMENT

Shawn Paul:

Over the course of my career, I have worked at various locations and at various levels. At each location, there was at least one person, either my boss or my support staff or my client, who was great at asking the right questions. I dedicate this book to those astute thinkers, who asked the right questions and led my knowledge journey. My thanks goes to Joe Abdullah at Crystal Financial Group, Neil Anderson at General Motors and Bruce Fishburn at Parker Hannifin for their suggestions and thoughts.

As I started writing this book, I knew that it was a long task. However, I enjoyed every bit of it. I thank my wife, Sarah, and my kids, Crystal and Jonathan, for their support and understanding during long evenings and late nights that I was up at my computer.

I thank Aditya at Blue Rose Publishers for working with me over the long haul on this publication.

Prof. Wilfred Paul:

It was an interesting experience writing this book at Blue Rose Publishers. Thanks to my wife, Prema for her support during the project.

Shawn Paul
Prof Wilfred Paul

CONTENT

PART 1

BUSINESS NEEDS

&

SUPPLY CHAIN

CHAPTER 1

INTRODUCTION

"You can't manage today's business, through yesterday's eyes"

–Lonnie Sciambi on Supply Chain planning.

In today's market, businesses are changing at lightning speed. Take for instance, Amazon. The transformation has been phenomenal from a bookseller in the 1990s to the range of products sold today. Amazon is still growing with the current market cap above US $800 billion with the acquisition of Whole Foods and the upcoming direct sales planned in pharmaceuticals. In 1996, Amazon had 151 employees and a revenue of US $5 million, scaling to US $8 Billion and 8000 employees in just 4 years. Another example is Walmart. The company was founded in 1962, 34 years before Amazon and has gone through generations of changes. Walmart has grown from a small Southern big box retailer to an online competitor for Amazon in many sectors. In India, Flipkart, that is 81.3% owned by Walmart, holds a 51% online market-share against 13% share of Amazon in fashion goods. This rate of business change is not unique to only big businesses.

A similar microcosm of change is evident in small enterprises as well. Let's view this small business change through the lens of business outlook in the Southeast Michigan area industry.

In the 1990s and 2000s, the area had just realized that its nearly 100-year reliance on the Auto industry was not sustainable going forward. On a cold wintry day in Dec 2002, the author and his partners had gathered in the Crystal Financial Group (CFG) offices in Farmington Hills, Michigan for a client meeting. CFG was a consulting services company and a business brokerage, working with private capital and assisting entrepreneurs in setting up small to medium cap companies. Joe Abdullah, our client was a towering man and someone who was not afraid of new challenges. He had spent many years at Ford Motor Co. at various levels. But that day, he was worried about the short-term future of retailing, now that the area had started showing signs of distress. The future looked very bleak for Southeast Michigan, and especially, Metro Detroit.

The brewing crisis for our client was that a string of retail business units that had just launched in the Saline/Ypsilanti area, south of Ann Arbor, Michigan, were not growing as planned. The problem was bigger than small business profitability. Many larger auto suppliers in the area had started to consolidate for maintaining their global market share and to focus on new markets, where China growth was just happening. But in the small and medium enterprises (SMEs) this situation was very dire. Retail businesses and auto parts suppliers were scrambling to reinvent themselves.

This need for constant change and business reinvention is universal, across the country and across the globe. It is regardless, whether the changes are due to an internal drive such as at Amazon or due to external forces such as in the early 2000s in Southeast Michigan. Companies are realizing that this lightning rate of business change is the new norm. They are realizing that the path and solutions from the earlier years, with incremental changes will not work going forward. The rapid changes from 2000s in Southeast Michigan, are happening everywhere, to businesses large and small.

Critical to this change, is to stay relevant in today's market. How do you provide customer value when customer preferences and the rules of value itself are changing? The question is still the same, regardless of the business size. The author had the unique opportunity to work in this change catalyst process with small and mid cap businesses as a consultant at CFG and in his career at Fortune 500 companies in their supply chain process. Thanks to the questions and wisdoms of industry experts, such as Joe Abdulla, a revolutionary and systematic approach was developed at CFG to leverage the supply chain. The result was an inside-out change in the business model and the creation of a market driven solution. Repositioning

Core question??

established businesses is a hard task. But over the course of time, a bold new pattern had emerged.

ROLE OF SUPPLY CHAIN   *Definition (tradition)*

Popular literature survey will describe Supply Chain as "the sequence of all activities to plan, control and execute the product (or service) delivery, starting from the first step to the last step". Therefore, Supply Chain Management (SCM) is the ability of a business to coordinate and manage multiple and legally separated entities in delivering valuable end-products or services to the customer. In addition, there is a vast flow of information, along with material, service components and financial enablers in a typical supply chain network. For a successful business, supply chain planning needs to be done end to end, covering all steps of business and incorporating all business functions including R&D, sales, service, procurement and other functions for net benefit to the organization. Therefore, as the enabler of the cash to cash business cycle, supply chain is the backbone of the company (Hong, 2015).

The importance of supply chain in the success of the business cannot be understated. Choosing and executing the right supply chain can make or break a business. A successful business may be as small as the newspaper delivery route for a teenager or a trillion-dollar cap business like Apple. A bankrupt business may be similar in scale to Kodak films, the giant film manufacturer from yesteryears, that disappeared a few years ago or the many street corner restaurants that seem to change names and ownerships every year. If the business is not scalable to the revenue it generates, it is not viable.

The benefits of optimizing the supply chain function is the first step in ensuring the right alignment of the supply chain to the business function. Most businesses can save substantial dollars with small changes in their supply chain layout. No owner or manager will say no to these additional savings on the bottom line, since the operation will have minimal changes. In simple terms, the benefit of stand-alone optimization of your supply chain to align to the business needs is a low hanging fruit and companies should take immediate steps to realize it. Typical savings from these optimization initiatives lead to better competitive costs and other advantages. Some commonly realized advantages are:

1. Improved product quality.

2. Cost minimization, while maintaining customer service level or rightsizing service.

3. Improved lead time and customer delivery commitments.

4. Growth in market share while capturing unique supply chain variations.

5. Ability to use distributed manufacturing and/or warehousing to satisfy distributed customer markets.

While this book focusses on the strategic planning of business and supply chain, here are some examples of supply chain cross functional optimization that are published as case study of savings that are well known in the industry. Companies like Walmart, IBM and Parker Hannifin have developed cost competitive advantages using optimized supply chain. Even if supply chain is practiced in isolation, these local results are remarkable.

1. IBM has taken the supply chain inventory concept to another level. In the last decade, IBM commissioned an Inventory Study on Asset Management to optimize its costs. The aim was to compete with new entrants in the consulting field, where IBM was an established but expensive player. Based on the study, IBM created a new inventory model to standardize the skill set "inventory" of its consultants. With a new inventory skills model, employees from different departments with identical skills can be used to staff new projects and thus the people inventory becomes centralized. IBM saved $750 million and improved revenues with this new strategy. (Lin, 2000)

2. In the late 1990s, the big three big-box retailers, Walmart, K-mart and Target ruled the market. While K-mart had twice the number of stores and 50% higher revenues than Walmart in 1987, Walmart continued to invest in advanced supply chain, including cutting out wholesalers,

building regional and local distribution centers, creating its own fleet, data linking the point of sale systems to order management and creating key partnerships with major suppliers like Proctor and Gamble. With higher priced slower moving goods, higher operating costs and lower profits, K-mart lost market competitiveness (Schoenberger, 2002) and filed for chapter 11 bankruptcy in 2003.

3. When Parker Hannifin decided to enter into the hybrid refuse truck business, there was a competition between Eaton Corporation and Parker, for getting first entry into the market. The author and his team were responsible to acquire and integrate a producer for hydraulic accumulator (a key component for hybrids) into the Parker group of companies. This gave Parker the edge over Eaton in the race to deliver new refuse trucks.

4. Another operational example for supply chain is Apple. Apple in Japan was able to lockdown the supply chain of DRAMs. The 2011 earthquake crisis was a painful tragedy of people and business losses in Japan. However, after the earthquake, Apple was able to recover and lead the market, when other smart phone companies like Google Pixel had to stop production due to the lack of DRAM memory resources. Apple was successful and grew its market share. (Morgenstern, 2011)

Overall the Best in Class supply chain leaders led every industry with a minimum of 5% higher margins, with 15% less inventory (less working capital), 25% less cash cycle times (again, less working capital) and 15% better perfect orders, according to the AMR study of supply chain[1]. The supply chain focus to date is to optimize towards a peak performance and reduced waste.

However, the central theme of this book, the business innovation process is the "SMART Supply Chain". Supply chain, the backbone of the company, becomes the key aspect of the disruption and reincarnation of

---

[1] https://www.researchgate.net/publication/316617314_COMPARING_SUPPLY_CHAIN_PERFORMANCE_METRICS_WITH_ORGANIZATIONAL_EXCELLENCE_PERFORMANCE_METRICS

the company. This book is intended to showcase how companies have understood the business needs of the market place and rebuilt themselves using this in their reinvention process. As you traverse through the pages, you will see trends that will enable your own rediscovery for your company.

THE ORGANIZATION OF THE BOOK

The book is divided into three parts. In part one, the background and fundamentals of this innovative approach are laid out. Chapter 2 focuses on the innovation patterns to enable your discovery of new customer value. Chapter 3 is crucial in that it identifies the toolbox of SMART supply chain strategies that help analyze and grow the business innovation.

Part two is the supply chain strategies for new business models. There we focus on the supply chain needs and characteristics inherent in each business. Business case studies cover a range of companies, from the tech savvy, Apple to product leaders such as Rolls Royce Engines, from small enterprises such as Car wash/Gas stations to market leaders such as Proctor & Gamble. Each industry and marketplace has its unique challenges. These challenges are discussed, and the common tools are explored throughout for each business model.

Part 3 covers the future of supply chain. Business innovations, such as toolbox, are best done in group workshops or as an iterative continuous improvement process. This iterative process enables the current business to thrive while the changes are implemented, so that the new business model does not kill the existing business line. Part 3 lays the foundation for the supply chain improvement journey.

This book provides the bold and revolutionary strategy that the CFG leadership developed for creating a breakthrough in business model plan refocusing on new supply chain and building new customer value propositions. Many clients have started the supply chain realignment process as a planning action, while some have started this journey after an external business change is in the air. Some common business changes that are experienced by these clients include the following situations:

- Setting up your new product line or a new business.

- Establishing a new cutting-edge improvement in business.

- Start of a new M & A process, with right sizing each business function.

- Competitive review.

- Entering a new marketplace or global diversification.

- Diversification or divesting of the business.

- Everyday need for improved cost structure, especially in response to new competitive threats in the marketplace.

FLOW OF THE BOOK

The book is set up in a funnel flow format, with three rings. The top ring is part 1 of the book, where the business needs of the organization are explored. Part 1 sets the stage for the business plans that go hand in hand with the supply chain plan. The middle ring is part 2, where the supply chain is tied to the business models. In business, the supply chain inspirations can come from startups to manufacturing companies. Each model has a unique advantage that will form the basis of the brand.

The bottom ring is part 3 on the execution of this strategy, the bull's eye. Each part builds on the previous part, until the final chapter. The focus of this final chapter is to tie the benefits of supply chain to the business transition plan and the business models.

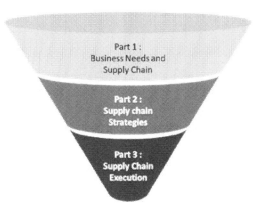

Figure 1.1: Layout of the book

The book is written visually, with several figures to help explain the concepts. Research has shown that visual presentations empower the reader to solve their unique problems using the creative and the logical sides of the brain. Author's experiences and business case studies are presented in each situation.

WHO WILL BENEFIT FROM THIS BOOK

This book is written for those who have realized that the incremental change of yesteryears will not work in the business of the future. The book is made especially for you, if you are:

- A Business leader, who is not satisfied with the status quo.

- A Chief Supply Chain Officer (CSCO), responsible for the strategic decisions of the company. CSCO is a board member, increasingly common today in many companies.

- A Cross functional thinker, pushing the limits of change.

- The Supply Chain professional or Business planner.

- A Supply Chain academic, exploring new areas.

- And anyone ready for a business change and looking for the tools for this change.

These leaders and specialists have realized that incremental change is not enough. Since the backbone of every company is supply chain, this is a transformational change in business. Businesses 100 years ago, underwent disruption every other generation. For instance, General Motors, till recently, was largely the same company assembled by the Chief architect, Billy Durant. Billy had the foresight to create a multi-brand holding company, assembling several companies from Buick to Chevy from 1904 to 1920. Change came to GM after losing the volume sales leadership to Toyota and VW. Now, GM is led by a successful female executive and the company is evolving and making tough business decisions every day.

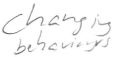 *changing behaviors*

Today most businesses change business plans at least a few times in one generation. Many companies that were household names just a few years ago, have rapidly evolved into new entities or disappeared from the business landscape. These include names such as Blockbuster Video going out of business, since it did not accept the new business model of video streaming, and the onset of Netflix. Or Kodak going out of business, due to the invention of the digital camera that required no film.

Most books on business models, identify a top down strategy on how to remake and reposition your business. They are missing the grass roots market driven process of how change can be dramatic, starting at the market place. This book combines the business strategy with the inside out thinking to yield a bold original approach for the reinvention of your business. *important*

The challenge for business is how it can become a disruptive business innovator. Companies that were once on the leading edge, are now in trouble. Today, with the international cost of capital being low, there are low barriers to a new business entry. So, the benefits of being an incumbent business may be short-lived. In the vehicle manufacturing business, Tesla has established itself very quickly compared to the likes of General Motors and Toyota. Many new decisions, such as an all-electric full line of cars, that the established OEs are planning, may be a result of this competitive threat. These changes may come from changes in customer lifestyle or from new business models. In the baby boomer generation, a new car ownership was the key aspiration, after affordability was established. However, in the millennial generation, car subscription services, such as Zip car are popular for short term use and ride sharing for every day commuting. As the trend continues, only time will tell, if car ownership will reduce drastically.

New technology is driving new business models every day. These models can represent new opportunities and threats to your business. Companies such as ABB are investing heavily in IoT, the technology for Internet of Things, where every gadget and location is digitally connected in the factory and every facility management is conditionally programmed with maintenance alerts. New challenges and new product releases are killing outmoded ones.

Stephen Elop, the Nokio CEO, had to make such a choice in 2011. He described it with the allegory of the burning platform where the protagonist had to jump off a burning oil rig into the freezing North Sea or wait for the burn. This is the case, where the change or the business necessity comes in late and cannot save the company or the product platform. Stephen was concerned on the viability of the Nokia native platform and alternatively, the delayed decision to choose one of the non-homegrown platforms such as the ioS, Android or Windows for the upcoming Nokia phones.

Simple product differentiation and global expansion are not working as complete strategies any more. The contents for this book are presented as a journey for disruptive business models. So, BON VOYAGE on your journey.

***

Chapter 2

Business models
and
Supply chain

Laxshman Singh is a hotel turnaround entrepreneur in Michigan. Known as "Lucky" Singh to his friends, he was looking for new hotel business in Southeast Michigan. His purchase, a branded 110 room hotel in Kalamazoo, Michigan for US $5 million was a bargain. Kalamazoo had large business clients, but this hotel property had anemic sales. He knew the two main yardsticks for hotel business viability, the occupancy rate and the ADR, were doing well in Kalamazoo. Occupancy rate is the percentage of occupied rooms in an average night and ADR was the average daily rate, since corporate customers and walk-in customers pay different room rate. However, his purchase property with its occupancy rate at 55% was extremely low and not sustainable. The hotel was situated on a highway exit, but due to competition, the highway traffic was not sufficient for full volume operation. Lucky had done his market research, the property was under 10 years old, relatively new in hotel years. Comparable hotels were running at 75% or better occupancy rate and so the local business potential was there. So what was missing, was the business plan that can bridge the gap. How can Lucky improve and reposition his business?

He could always remove the brand name and go with a generic brand. Or move the hotel from moderate upscale to budget hotel, with a badge such as Travelodge or Baymont inn. Both these actions will reduce the operating cost and help cover the monthly expenses. He could then further cut costs by insourcing room services, since Travelodge does not require staffing levels, such as with Holiday Inn, or Fairfield (by Hilton). However, in the long run, with the ADR drop, 25% discount for budget brands over his current brand name, he will lose money. So, he decided a big move with considerable additional investment. He purchased the neighboring property, created a ballroom and signed up for corporate accounts, jumping in with a fully leveraged business with both feet. His risk paid off, when he reached ADR at $95 a night and 80% occupancy in the next year. His business became a top grossing hotel in its category for Kalamazoo for the next two years.

While Lucky's task was laudable risk taking, his brother, Harpreet Singh was in deep trouble. His stamping company in Sterling Heights lost its contract with Chrysler, since the sales volume had dropped with the declining sales of the Chrysler Town & Country vans. Harpreet Singh, known as Happy Singh to his friends, was very unhappy. Enclosed are some of the alternative business models that Happy Singh considered, that were proposed by CFG.

Before we start on the business model, we must understand the structure of these models. A company's activities can be divided into Internal facing operations and Customer operations. Some examples of these operations for an automotive company such as Ford, are the plant and sourcing operations, that are internal to the organization and the dealer retail and warranty support that are Customer or external operations. Business research has clearly shown that companies that are closer to the customer and better understand the customer needs, get better margins on their products. These businesses can compete on cost and perceived value, compared to other businesses that do not have such a contact. With direct sales, the same enterprise can manage the customer interaction.

On the internal side, the business can manufacture the entire product or service by itself. The enterprise can also outsource some or all the activities to its suppliers with the final product sold to customers. These choices are shown in Figure 2.1. Companies have a mix of internal operations levels and customer contact levels. Many startups outsource both these streams during the startup phase, and slowly build competency in-house. Mass producers such as Auto companies, have substantial internal operations. Channel experts manage the customer interaction better, while end to end "Full house" type of companies, manage the internal and customer operations within the company.

Cómo pasar de high-low a high-high

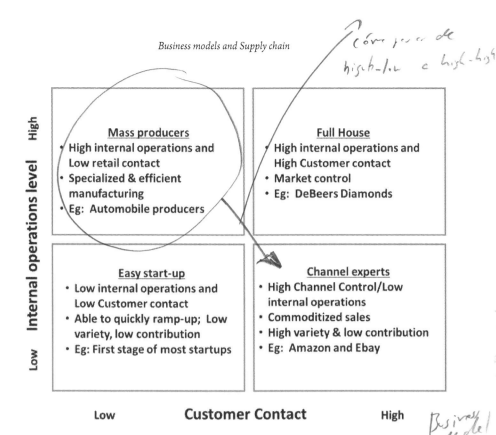

Figure 2.1: Comparison of channel ownership

and

Internal operations levels

Business model Canvas

Now let's consider the template tool for laying out the business model. The purpose is to establish a common terminology. Many business model books have different templates that are popular in their working circles. One such elaborate modelling tool is the Business model canvas, proposed by Alexander Osterwalder and Yves Pigneur (Osterwalder, 2010). In the book, Alex proposes a 7-box template for documenting and evaluating business models. These 7 box categories include: Key Activities, Key Resources, Key Partnerships, Value Propositions, Customer segments, Channels and Customer Relationships. This business model is based on the foundation that the cost and revenue streams, need to match to make a viable company. This is a good tool for a full business model evaluation.

However, in our analysis of SMART supply chain, the following simplified template has been the most effective. The business model should be separated to three streams. Answering the questions for each pillar will populate the details. A sample of the questions for these three streams are shown below. The three-pillar model for the business modelling includes the following

INTERNAL FACING OPERATIONS:

- What are the key in-house operations and outsourced operations?

- How do these operations add value to the end product or service?

- What are the processes to decide the flow of Internal facing operations?

- How are production, sourcing and other operations handled?

- Are all operations driven by the common forecast? Who is accountable for this forecast?

- What are the key priorities of the Internal facing operations?

VALUE PROPOSITIONS:

- What adds value to the end customer? What is the unique value that your product offers to the customer? (Typical uniqueness includes: newness, performance, customization, everything done at one stop, design, brand/status, price, cost reduction, risk reduction, accessibility, convenience/usability etc.).

- How does your company's value proposition compare with its competition?

CUSTOMER OPERATIONS:

- What are the customer inputs? How do customer operations assist in sales and customer services? (This includes the customer experience, customer contact, dedicated personal assistance, self-service, automated service, communities, co-creation etc.)

- What are the different customer segments that your business is targeting? (Examples: Mass market, niche market, segmented, multi-sided etc).

- How does the customer operations bring in value?

Figure 2.2 shows the Business model house template that we will use for the supply chain strategy evaluation throughout the rest of this book.

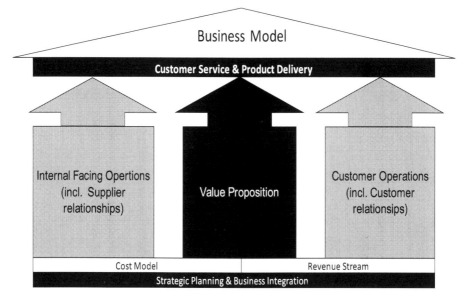

Figure 2.2: The 3 Pillar house template for business model synthesis

Now that we have established a template for synthesizing business models, let's look at business strategies, along with the business models. In the age of startups and unicorns, it is just a matter of time when every industry and every business will get disrupted.

Enclosed is a sample of the top disruptive models in the industry today. The models are presented here, for an understanding of the business plan layout for disruptive business innovators. Each model will give you an insight of how the customer value is being redefined. Later in part 2, we will discuss how the company can plan for changes and what supply chain actions are necessary for the transition.

A sample of the top disruptive models are discussed below. Other models will be introduced when the supply chain strategies are discussed in part 2.

TECH DISRUPTION MODEL

No business structure has undergone as much disruption as that in the hi-tech industry. Hi-tech has been fast changing with short product cycles, and with the rapid flow of new products in constant disruption. For an in-depth review, let's take the eReader market. Book sales were driven by print and the market was evenly divided between the three leading book sellers in the early 2000s. Borders, Barnes & Nobles and Amazon had established their territories and market share. But Amazon does not have brick and mortar stores and was handicapped in book sales. So, in the classic tech disruption move, Amazon introduced the Kindle reader with new and unique advantages. The customer could now read on the go and take their whole library along with them in one Kindle reader device. Until then, the leading brick and mortar booksellers, relied on face to face interaction, convenience and their footprint of many bookstores for sales growth.

In fast reaction, Barnes & Noble put a special team together and launched a superior product, the Nook, in record time. However, Borders was late to the game, and their response for an eReader in 2010, was too late to catchup and Borders lost market share. Eventually, with the market shift, Borders filed for bankruptcy. Amazon has a high title count, but many readers still prefer the Barnes & Nobles' Nook reader. The business model for the Barnes and Noble Nook is shown in the Figure 2.3.

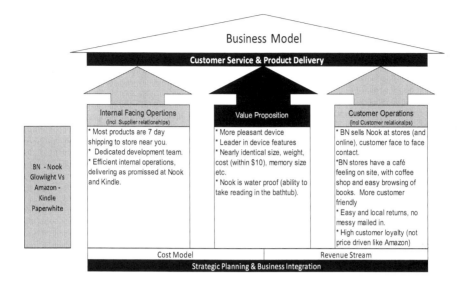

Figure 2.3: Business model for the Barnes and Noble, Nook Glow light

(Barnes&Nobles, 2018)

A key takeaway should be the method of disruption and the execution of the disruption at Amazon. A similar tech interrupter was Hyundai Automotive in India. In India, the air quality and fog warning had caused the Indian Supreme Court to restrict certain vehicle types in New Delhi, India's capital city and ban diesel vehicles above 2-liter diesel in late 2015. While most Indian, U.S. and European auto companies fought the restriction in court, Hyundai delighted its customers with newer clean engine features, new gasoline engine vehicles with fuel economy better than diesels, higher torque in smaller engines, fog lamps and other technology options, positioning the company as a tech leader and thus rapidly rising from 5th to 2nd position in sales volume.

We will review the supply chain strategies for the hi-tech disruptor model in the part 2 of the book.

OWNERSHIP VERSUS SHARING ECONOMY

Another disruption opportunity in customer value is the new "sharing economy". A popular concept, especially among millennials is the willingness and ability to rent major items, rather than the traditional

√ Sharing economy

model of full ownership. Zipcar has perfected this in major metro areas. In these areas, cars are available to "share" or rent by the hour or by the day. So, customers use the public transportation or carpooling for day to day work, while Zip car rentals are available for hour to hour rental, on as-needed basis.

The cost of sharing and the additional maintenance management are driving features, which companies such as Rolls Royce and Hilti have used in their business model. Rolls Royce Engines has created a Care store business where the maintenance of its engines is managed by Rolls Royce. Since engine maintenance and life cycle management are big competency issues for airlines, this offers airlines the ability to outsource the entire engine maintenance operations to Rolls Royce. The supply chain strategies for the on-demand rental sharing economy and Hilti's unique business of tool rentals is discussed in detail in part 2.

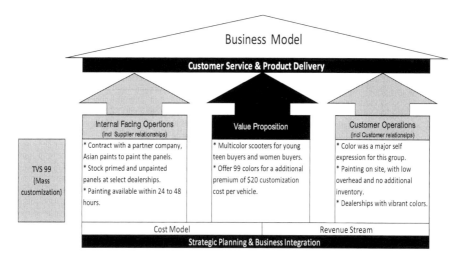

Figure 2.4: Business model for TVS99 – Color options on the go
(Shah, 2016)

A variation to this on-demand availability is that companies such as TVS, a popular scooter company in India and South America, has offered 99 custom color options in the market. This is especially attractive for teens and younger women, who can choose the scooter color at the dealership for custom delivery within 48 hours. Primed panel of scooter frames are sent to the dealerships and are on standby for the customers' color choices. When the customer chooses a color option, the panels are shipped to the supplier facility at Asian Paints, where the painting is completed and ready for the customer delivery the next day. The business model for TVS99 is shown in Figure 2.4. The supply chain required for this execution is discussed in detail in part 2.

MARKET SEGMENTERS

↑ General Motors and Tesla

Many new businesses start up in a new area as a niche marketer, such as Amazon as the online bookseller, or Tesla as the premium brand electric car company. In Tesla's case, the car companies refused to take it seriously in the first few years. This is mostly because of General Motors' experience in launching and failing at the electric option in the 1980s. The car companies had written off the electric car due to cost, where the electric cars were substantially higher than the current internal combustion models and "range anxiety", where the electric car owners did not drive far for the risk of running out of charge. The author was given the small electric car for market review and testing in Asia. With the state of charge (or distance to empty) at 100 kilometers, the car test was limited to about 40 or so kilometers from the electric charging station for the ability to return without running dry.

Tesla has built the business model on the electric car, and by making the car popular, is likely to drive the entire marketplace to electric vehicle. Elon Musk, the founder of Tesla, has established sourcing in China, created a thriving electric charging business to extend driving range, developed a specialized supply base, created a unique assembly process and set up a business driven completely on preorders for cars (at least initially). We will discuss the business model and the supply chain in the following chapters.

ECOSYSTEM+ DISRUPTOR

A popular model for disruption is the ecosystem+ model. In this model, the company binds the customer with its unique features and locks in the long-term marketing potential. A typical example of this action is the phone service with Android or Apple. If the initial purchase is made, the customers are locked in for the length of their contract. Apple is an expert player of this model. Apple has managed customer experience by creating its own stores. If your apple computer or phone has a hardware issue, your only option is the Apple store. Some other electronic stores will be able to do light maintenance on software, but substantial troubleshooting work is not available other than in the Apple store. We will discuss the supply chain strategies and business strategies options that Apple pursued and if these models will work for your business.

NEW MARKETPLACE

Air bed and breakfast founders, Brian, Joe and Nathan travelled to DC to attend the Presidential inauguration ceremony for President Obama. They were looking for marketing opportunities for their startup, Air bed and breakfast or Airbnb for short. All hotels in the DC area were full, giving them an ideal opportunity for marketing to people looking for unusual places to stay. A restaurant manager who was being evicted from his residence, gave them a place to stay and they were able to find additional hosts for Airbnb in the few empty rooms upstairs in the same building. In a funny way of a story reminiscent of the Christmas story, with no room in the inn, they passed out flyers asking for people to rent their extra rooms. The business boomed with an on-air endorsement in Good Morning America, for unusual places to stay for the event.

Today Airbnb offers the world's largest collection of lodging accommodations. As an Airbnb customer, I know that what I see is what I will get. So that curation gives me the confidence to stay in unusual places. Airbnb offers hosts the opportunity to earn the extra cash for their unused rooms. The supply chain for Airbnb requires local representatives to curate the experience, so that you will get the same experience that was promised.

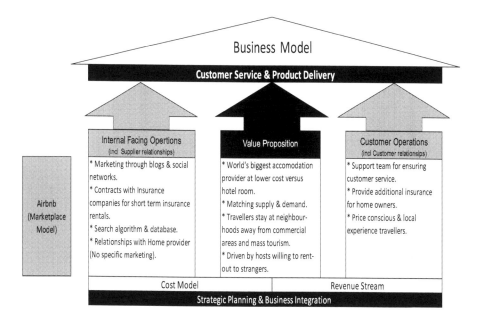

Figure 2.5: The Airbnb Business Model

(Bailey, 2018)

FREEMIUM DISRUPTIVE MODEL

Freemium is an attractive strategy, combining the free sampling and a premium paid service offered together. This business model provides an opportunity for a captured customer base, using the free basic functionality. Freemium is really a tiered business structure where the base functionality or service is offered free of cost, while the add-ons are priced with each additional feature. LinkedIn is a great example of the Freemium model, where a clear majority of the professionals maintain a profile and additional services such as job seeking, or sales marketing are priced at a premium.

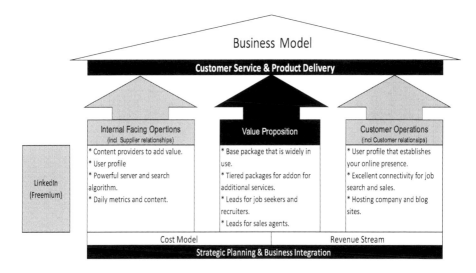

Figure 2.6: Business model for LinkedIn
(LinkedIn website, 2018)

By now, you would have seen the disruption opportunity in business with these new business models. We shall discuss several other models and their supply chain strategies in part 2. Each strategy has a unique opportunity in the marketplace, given the right conditions. In part 2, we will also see that your business may have all the ingredients to drive a new business model, with a little strength and conditioning in an area or two.

✻✻✻

Chapter 3

Developing the smart toolbox

It was in Oct 2006, when I (Shawn) met Mr. Basky at our CFG Offices in Farmington Hills, Michigan. Known to his friends as "Nascar" Basky, he was a trained Chef from Singapore and cooked for several NASCAR legends in Charlotte. Basky was a versatile chef, who came to the Southeast Michigan area with a dream. His dream was to own his own restaurant.

Over the next three months, our team showed him several restaurants for sale in the Metro area, while he wowed us by his range of global culinary talents. He could make everything from Brazilian strip steaks, to Chinese Chicken Kung Pao, and a Southern deep-fried dessert to Indian curry without batting a wink. We were astonished by his width of culinary skills, his customer service and his can-do attitude. Since Basky was new to the business of running a restaurant, he needed a business partner. Having dabbled in restaurant business before, we knew that boutique restaurants lived and died by the chef's talents. If the chef is no more, the restaurant is no more. Excited to have a notable talent, we joined forces with him to open a Fusion restaurant in Troy, Michigan. Now, Troy was a growing suburb in Oakland County, with major auto suppliers located there. Oakland County was the wealthiest county in the US in 2006. So, with the office crowd in place, the business lunch market was strong. The area had many young couples with dual income and no kids. So, with the right dinner ambiance, the dinner crowd potential was strong too.

Once the business started, things were a different story. Our features and options were limited and our toolbox for experimentation was limited. The first hurdle was the liquor license, this was controlled by city of Troy. Our only option was to offer wine catering from the store next door at a corking fee, until the next batch of liquor licenses were available in few months. Since wine menu was a major revenue, we were limited to half our potential. The second was lunch crowd, most of the local offices had tie-ups for lunch delivery, so we had to fill volume to make up for flow.

The long and short of the experience is that our supply chain and business SMART toolbox was not strong. Developing the tools from scratch, we had to invest in a delivery truck, to fill kitchen space. A separate catering and food delivery menu were needed as well. But with constant innovation, Basky was growing into his second location within a year.

The tools for the SMART supply chain are a unique driver for innovative disruption. Each tool fit a framework of SMART supply chain strategy. The elements of this framework are:

S—Sensing Demand

M—Market driven

A—With an Analytical basis (and a systematic approach)

R—Real world, real time solutions, driven across functions

T—Toolbox based approach, for business experimentation

As we have seen before, the business internal needs and customer needs are supply chain driven for creative disruption. At the Troy restaurant, the first need for adaptation was sensing demand. Starting as a Fusion restaurant, attracted a wide group of customers. However, some customers felt that the width of fusion recipes was not enough. So, we provided delivery service from our competition on Fridays. For a revenue model, we adopted a subscription service, where a steady monthly subscription was offered. Sensing demand and anticipation of customer trend is the key element of the SMART supply chain.

Secondly the business is market driven. The delivery service was a market driven change and required a separate P & L. Every customer that visited the restaurant, was encouraged to put their business card into a jar for special promotions. Each business card had a customer's favorite dish from the restaurant, or the favorite request, and once-a-week customers could win one of their favorites. This was one of the several market feedback mechanisms.

On Mondays, the team analyzed what food is to be sold in what quantities and kitchen scheduling wait times for each food category. Based on these numbers, some food may be dropped from the next menu change. Eating out is a special experience, and we wanted to ensure our regular customers choose us every time or at least most of the time for their dinner experience. So, we ensured the right ambiance with live exotic instrumental music for every dinner. Every change was wetted for the real world. This included sampling the competition and identifying their strengths, done through a cross functional team. In the Troy restaurant, the steering team with the Head Chef, the Business General Manager, the delivery van service manager and the managing partner discussed every plan and every change before implementation.

Big data and analytics are essential to any business. The job of the analytics is to convert the tons of data that is available into meaningful insights. If the data conversion is delayed in processing into actionable insights, the business will quickly get overwhelmed with mounds of useless data.

A structured process is necessary for the extraction of insights from the big data. Our rule of thumb for the small business is to collect the total weekly sales by item in an excel spreadsheet, along with the wait times. One member of the steering team will post process and present the insights to the cross functional team. Large businesses with more resources will employ specialized Oracle or SAP data collection modules that extract information from the ERP, APM and other modules on a continuous stream; Data plotting is available for each day and each week, going back to the last quarter. Beyond the last quarter, the raw data storage will be cumbersome and can be recycled. The supply chain analytics should cover the following areas:

K PI's *The Smart Supply chain*

Internal facing operations	Value Proposition	Customer operations
Sourcing Production Warehouse Transportation Planning	Competitor Values Customer Perception Value Enablers	Point of sale Customer information Channel information Product Delivery Return

Table 3.1: Scope of Supply chain tools for disruptive action

Supply chain as The Plan-Source-Make-Deliver-Return process

THE SMART TOOL BOX

Now we come to the review of the SMART toolbox. The toolbox is not exotic collection of tools, but rather a carefully picked tool set of strategies that transform business models. Each strategy is unique for the outcome it requires from the business. The strategies cover the bigger picture of actions that are required in the disruptive business. The toolbox and its layout is presented below. Later in part 2, we will see the application examples of how this tool box can be used for the company business plan.

The SMART tool box is laid out in a similar structure to the business model template that we have discussed in the previous chapter. The business toolbox is again divided into three pillars. The left pillar is the Internal facing operations pillar and it covers the in-house and virtual activities of the company. In the business planning stages, the division between what activities are in-house and what are outsourced is going to be decided. This strategic decision will be done within this Internal facing operations pillar. The cost structure of the company and the value creation are done from the center towards the left of the business tool box template, that is starting from the planned value proposition to the Internal facing operations that are necessary to realize this customer value.

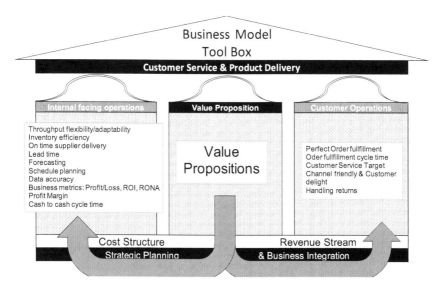

Figure 3.1: Value propositions flowchart to identify the Internal facing and Customer operation needs.

The right side of the tool box has the Customer operations. The revenue stream is generated from the customer operations, based on the value that the company offers to its customers in the product or service offering. The choice of the internal and customer operations should support the value proposition for the company. Figure 3.1 shows the outward flow of the value proposition into the business functions.

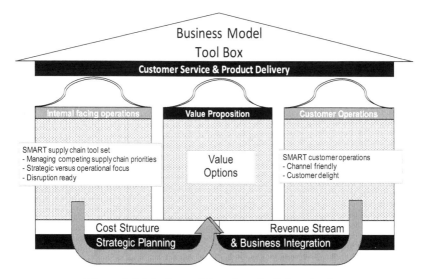

Figure 3.2: The Inward flowchart for Value Options

The creation of the right functions in the organization, enables the realization of the value proposition. But in our experience, it is very clear that certain businesses have an affinity to a business model and certain value options. If the business is fine-tuned to those options, the flow of the business and the strength of the brand are immensely increased. The process of realigning the business functions to the value propositions, gives a reward of alternate value options that the business can market going forward. This reverse flow is shown in Figure 3.2.

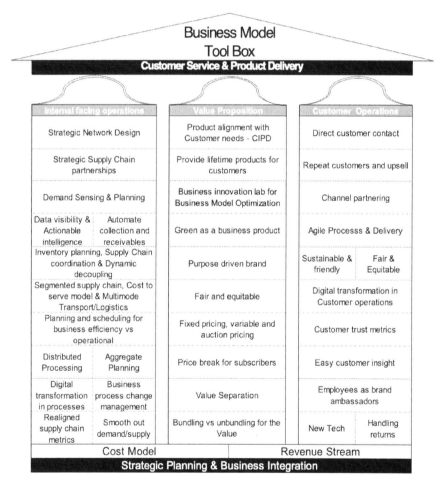

Figure 3.3: The SMART Supply Chain toolbox

Supply chain is a unique area in business and requires a cross functional toolbox for execution and a knowledge of the business priorities, along with the cross execution with other functions. First step is to review the business strategic competence. This decision is between what is to be kept as in-house core competence and what is to be outsourced as a virtual competence.

Every company wants to maintain control of the proverbial "secret sauce", the key ingredient that distinguishes your company's product offering from what is in the marketplace. This requires firm planning and drive to identify what resources to bring in house. For example, early in the product development and execution, Apple decided that they will control the design and customer experience. So, Apple installed a worldwide network of retail stores and a design office which managed new product launches very well. Assembly and component manufacture were outsourced to companies such as Foxconn and Samsung. More on the Apple business model and supply chain in part 2 of the book.

The SMART toolbox and elements of the supply chain are shown in the Figure 3.3. Each of the elements of the SMART toolbox will be explored in detail in the relevant business model. While, the strategic level of these tools are highlighted here, the operational level of supply chain cannot be missed. There are several other strategies for the day to day activities in the operational level of supply chain, and that will continue besides this strategic SMART toolbox.

CASE STUDY

As an introduction to the supply chain strategies, we present the case study of Johnson Controls. This case study is presented as a warm-up for the supply chain discussions to come.

Author (Shawn) and his team were tasked at Johnson Controls (now Adient plc), to setup seating for its new plant in Plymouth, Michigan. Johnson Controls & now, Adient is the world's largest producer of seats for a range of vehicles. The company has diversified from automotive seating into airplane seating as well, with its joint venture with Boeing.

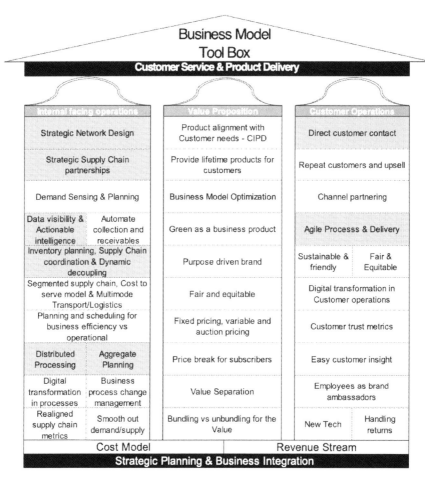

Figure 3.4: SMART toolbox & Strategic planning for Johnson Controls Seating
(Now Adient plc)

The SMART toolbox for Johnson Controls is shown in Figure 3.4. Six tools in Internal facing operations and two tools in customer operations were key elements for Johnson Controls strategy in 1995.

Being a leader in vehicle seating, Johnson Controls had a unique view of how to manage the business. Each vehicle seat design was unique. But the seat frame tubes and the lost foam cushion were common materials across all seats. Johnson Controls created a mechanism of *Aggregate planning*[2]. Seat build forecasts across multiple vehicles was combined to

---

[2] Each SMART toolbox element in action is shown in **bold & *italics text*** during the discussion.

procure the seat frames, belt buckle accessories and the foam required for each seat.

Location planning and logistics drop-off for each plant was decided based on OE plant location. With the best in class testing and development facility, Adient is in excellent shape for future business. Each business is managed by an account manager, who ensures the forecast visibility at the plant. **Strategic sourcing** and **network design** established the desirable location for the tier 2 suppliers. This was driven by a central sourcing team.

Careful **Inventory planning and Decoupling stock** was organized so that each plant capacity was laid out flexibly to accommodate capacity needs variation, based on fluctuating vehicle demand. Capacity and flow planning were based on the OE forecast, but with quick scalability up and down to 30% of volume. OE and supplier **Data visibility** was required for this dynamic scaling.

In addition, to maintain leadership, Johnson Controls decided to develop a premium line of seating in 1995, and thus separate itself from the run of the mill. Until that time, seat belts were anchored in the B-pillar, that separate the front row and the rear row of the car, for crash safety reasons. The company developed a new seat with the seatbelts integrated into the seat. This was especially useful since the seatbelts were clumsy and hard to use, when the seat is far ahead or way behind the B-pillar. Buckling the seat belt is less comfortable, since the seat belt wraps around you at an awkward angle, when the seat belt is pivoted from the B-pillar. This first of its kind seating was installed in the Chrysler Sebring convertible and was awarded the innovation award.

Each of these strategies enabled Johnson Controls to maintain leadership in the business. Johnson Controls was in manufacturing business, where the cost of entry was high in 1995. Now with the easy capital and the entry of new competition as a premise, let's move to part 2, where we will analyze how the business models shape the supply chain strategies. The business case tie-in for supply chain cases, such as Johnson Controls, will be presented in part 2 with an in-depth discussion.

***

PART 2

SUPPLY CHAIN
STRATEGIES
FOR DISRUPTORS

THE RED QUEEN PRINCIPLE

In today's competitive marketplace, the customer expectations are driving faster service, competitive cost and delivery accuracy. Businesses fulfill these terms through their supply chains. Therefore, these supply chains are in-turn evaluated on their metrics of delivery process and operational cost. Over time this has led to the lean practices in supply chain, where waste is targeted for elimination. Using the lean terminology, that originated from Japan, the three areas that are targeted are:

Muda: Operational Waste

Mura: Lack of smooth operations

Muri: Overscheduling of resources during operation

Supply chain efficiency has been a hot topic for many years. During the last decade, several Fortune companies invested in supply chain efficiency for stand-alone gains as a solution for cost reduction. Capital infrastructure projects covered state-of-the-art tech in supply chain, embracing logistics, warehouse management and inventory planning. Some projects concentrated on inventory levels and asset management. The key area of focus was vertical excellence in the supply chain domain.

Dow Chemicals, as a case study[3], had a cost reduction initiative covering multi-plant supply chain to drive down supply cost and to increase profitability margins. One-time individual savings and long-term cost efficiency were achieved. Dow utilized the supply chain data to get better risk management and increase profitability.

---

[3] https://www.gartner.com/doc/1760814/case-study-dow-chemical-uses

The other focus of supply chain has been the speed of operation. Amazon has moved from prime delivery in two days, to same day delivery in some select markets. This will undoubtedly have a catchup effect on the entire B2C marketplace. Supply chain speed with accurate delivery service is being prototyped with drones and other special options.

However, as the Red Queen had to run faster and faster to keep up with the changing scene in the Alice in wonderland children's fable, "Through the looking glass", repeating common actions for lean or greater speed, and its benefits, does not work as a business strategy. This gap is visible with companies such as Walmart and HP, the prior Supply Chain leaders, who are now in trouble. Business becomes an up and down cycle with the up times during business growth, leading to delivery competition and maximizing agility. During the down cycle, companies cut down supply chain features to minimize cost.

As we will see in the following chapters, these priorities are focused more on the company cost rather than on a business strategy and customer benefit. In the long term, such cost drivers, create a lag in supply chain capability to fulfill the business strategic need. The key questions, we should ask are:

1. What is the long-term business model and supply chain strategy? Can the supply chain capabilities be modified to meet the long term goals, instead of a simple cost reduction?

2. What is the plan for service/product launches and how does the supply chain support this plan?

3. How do we organize supply chain to benefit the customer and his/her perceived value?

4. Is there a strategy tie-in to the investment plan, providing a focus on developing the right supply chain skills for the company?

5. Do these strategies create another also ran business that is waiting for a disruption to happen?

6. Do these choices improve the competitive position or damage it?

Over the next chapters in part 2, we will explore customer value and how to target the supply chain strategy as a growth engine for the company. The unique requirements of the supply chain for each business model are explored in detail. Over the authors supply chain experience, there are many observations of strategies, and the history of strategic fit for each organizational supply chain. These observations are captured as a basic guideline, that are listed as rules. Each rule enables the reader to jumpstart a business model. These are box listed as shown below.

Let's start with the first rule. Every rule has an exception and is meant to be broken. Business reinventions happen when the you rise above the rule. The author encourages you to find your own creative path to a solution. So, the first rule is

Rule# 1	Break every rule. Situational adaptation is the more crucial tool.

Another feature that will be frequently presented are the small business examples of the business model. These may be presented in a format shown below, called the side bar.

Case of the 7-Eleven franchise

There are many convenience stores, and convenience store brands across the world. However, 7-Eleven brand is one of the most popular brands with more than 67000 stores in 17 countries.

The 7-Eleven stores were named that way to show the extended hours of operation from 7 am to 11pm. The store has a popular Slurpee drink in large sizes and a constant flow of new product introduction in the US. In Japan, the convenience store market is very competitive with several brands at each major cross section. Japanese 7-Eleven excel in convenience, with several airport locations, where you can purchase and heat your own food at a competitive price.

With so many stores and profit sharing at 59% with the corporation, the brand has established a value. However, at a product refresh rate at 70% every year, the constant change is the mantra for 7-Eleven franchisees.

CHAPTER 4

THE HI-TECH DISRUPTOR

"It takes a lot of hard work, to make things simple"

– Steve Jobs

The year was 2000. Steve Jobs had returned to Apple, a few years earlier. Apple was enjoying the success of the iMac. However, Steve was concerned. CDs were getting popular, especially with music sharing. Every DJ was bringing in their own cut of music in CDs and music sharing was trending. Steve was upset that the iMac did not have a CD player and all the music sharing was happening through Windows PCs. So, he was proposing to disrupt this scenario, and was looking for ideas.

A few years earlier a digital audio player, the Listen Up player, had won the innovation award at the CES show, but sold only 25 units. Another device, the Rio PMP, was reasonably successful during Christmas sales in 1998. However, there was a major lawsuit on illegal copying of music. And, there was a catch with each player. Each device had a limited memory, 16 to 32 MB, holding from 7 to 20 songs. So, after much research, Apple introduced the iTunes store in January 2001. For a company planning an entry into the digital audio market, this may sound like a backward strategy. But in the next few pages, we will explore this sequence and the clear master stroke that Steve had orchestrated.

The iTunes store overcame the first issue of music sales. Customers could now purchase music singles for as low as $0.99; and this became the branding for the product. Also, as expected, customers started building their own portable digital library of songs. So, when Apple launched the iPod, the digital audio player, in about eight months after iTunes store, it was an instant success. iPod was a mobile device with access to the iTunes product portfolio, songs and videos. Soon, iPod sales leapfrogged the loss of CD drives in iMac. Now with the new product and new strategy, iPod had become a brand sensation.

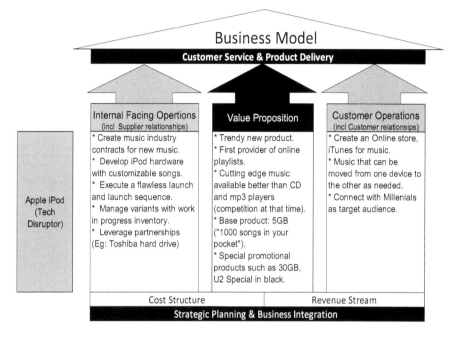

Figure 4.1: Business model for the iPod

(Business Model Navigator, 2019)

The iTunes store gave customers access to exclusive artist performances & new music, provided a convenient internet download for mobile library of songs, and the ability to transfer music digitally. Figure 4.1 shows the business model of the iPod brand. iPod was the first provider of online playlists. In due course, when it was clear that others were getting ready for similar music players and music services, Apple moved over to the iPhone. iPhone business overtook iPods by 2011. This is the next disruption that will be covered later. In each of the disruptions, the sequence of the supply chain events is the same, although the timelines are getting shorter and the new technology is coming in more rapidly.

The tech industry is full of such disruptions. In the past two decades, the rate of these disruptions is increasing and shows no sign of letting up. The window of opportunity for new products and new business is very short for each disruption. Each product in the marketplace, from Fitbit watches to hi-tech software solutions, introduced by the tech industry has been leap frogging each other. The range of such products in the tech industry, typically runs from software to hardware and electronics. In each case, the company can make the supply chain choices of in-house or outsourced competencies. The original tech company, Microsoft has evolved into more focused products. Now Microsoft does all their in-house software developments and outsources the hardware, such as Microsoft Surface tablets to preferred suppliers. Other tech companies, Intel and Oracle, Ebay and Hewlett Packard have similar options as well.

BUSINESS PRIORITIES & THE SMART TOOLBOX

Due to the unique fast evolving nature of product introductions in the hi-tech industry, the business organization and the supply chain priorities are unique. Businesses live or die by their new products and product features. Like the iceberg principle, where 90% of the floating iceberg is below the water line, a brand launch requires most of the Internal facing operations to go smoothly and is not visible to the public. There are many decisions that are required in the business planning preparation for a brand launch. The first is the key identities of the brand. In Apple's iPod, Steve Jobs had clearly laid out that the iPod should be a trendy new product. In addition, Steve identified that the customer should have a high-fidelity music with the same ease as listening to a radio or the CDs that came with the prebuilt "playlist". This resulted in the birth of the new idea, the online playlist, where you can have a customizable playlist that you can choose depending on your mood or who you are listening with. The second feature to leapfrog the other digital audio players, was that the iPod should have a 5GB memory. This translates to about 1000 songs that you can store on the iPod, compared to the 20 or so songs that were common in the earlier versions. Steve Jobs was open to special promotional versions of the iPod with higher capability than the base model as well.

Now let's tie in the business strategy (Figure 4.1) to the SMART toolbox, shown in Figure 4.2. Each of the business elements has a corresponding clear supply chain strategy for successful execution. The major planning activities are done in the Internal Facing Operations of the company. The first task is to identify if the product or service is to be made in-house and to what extent in-house. Companies such as Apple, prefer to outsource most of their hardware manufacturing.

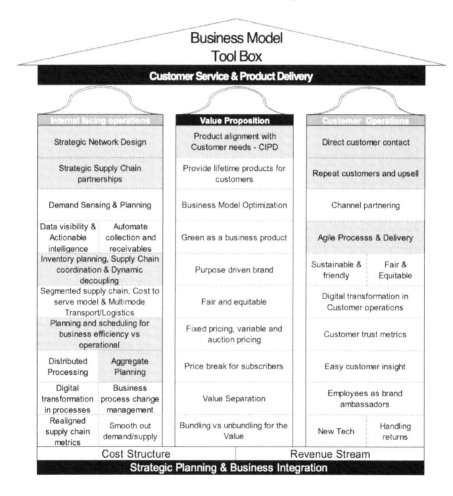

Figure 4.2: The SMART toolbox for the Hi-tech disruptor

Two companies with similar products may make substantially different decisions, based on this competency. For instance, Sony makes all their hardware components for their PlayStation product in-house. In contrast, Microsoft's popular Xbox team makes all the software development in-house. The hardware manufacturing for the Xbox is outsourced to Flexonics. This decision is based on the availability and the effectiveness of the in-house resources. Some other companies may have a hybrid strategy, where the base volume is made in-house and secondary fluctuating volume is sourced out, based on the cost structure. From the Chapter 1 discussion, when Parker Hannifin decided to make the hydraulic hybrid drive for garbage trucks, Parker procured a hydraulic accumulator company, so that it can keep the secret sauce in-house. In fact, the competition had submitted a request for a quote to Parker's accumulator division for their version of the same product. This is mostly the case, if the finances are available, and return on investment can be established for such a corporate purchase. The author and his team were key participants in the Parker decision.

Rule #2: **(Tom Peters)**	Do what you do best, outsource the rest. (Outsourcing strategy should be a strategic fit)

In the iPod business model, the Internal Facing Operations were led by Apple's hardware chief, Jon Rubinstein. As with most business tools, we will see shortly, the first decision that the team had to make was what was to be done in-house and what was to be done outside. Jon scaled up his design team, while making a contract with Toshiba for the key ingredient, the hard drive required for the iPod. Toshiba agreed to support the **Strategic Supply Chain Partnership**, with ample products, delivered on time to meet the demand. Typically, in hi-tech, the **Strategic Network Design**, where the supplier will setup plants and how the supply travel distance is managed will be a concern. But in Apple's case, because of the strength of the strategic partnership, the plant location was not a major concern. Toshiba would ensure the flow of materials for the new product.

The second supply chain strategy was the inventory planning that Apple executed to make this brand work. This requires a detailed discussion and we will review it in the next section in this chapter, along with the other inventory strategies, **Aggregate Planning** and **Agile Process Delivery**. The third supply chain strategy is the strategy and competence of ***First-time Readiness and Planning***. All companies are looking for a smooth product launch and getting the products without any issues to their customers during the launch. But hi-tech companies are hyper focused on this launch plan, since each product has a limited sales window. The customer perception from a launch can make or break the product. First time readiness for the launch is a key aspect for Hi-tech disruptor.

For the customer operations, Apple had just launched two locations for the Apple stores in 2001 and was planning on rapid expansion. The stores were devoted to having a ***Direct Customer Experience*** and ensuring that their needs were addressed, with first hand feed-back to Apple for fine-tuning regularly. The value proposition of the iPod was cleverly marketed through the "iPod people" campaign, connecting with the millennials. The target market for the iPod was the teens who before then had to carry big boom box stereos for listening to good music. Ads showing skating, biking and active youngsters and their music connected well with the teens. The market launch plan for the iPod, and the launch plans for the Fit bit or the Google Pixel phone are no different. We will discuss the other elements of the hi-tech product launch priorities, after the discussion on the SMART toolbox of supply chain processes in hi-tech.

Each of the supply chain priorities in hi-tech is tied to the toolbox processes in supply chain. The tool box of supply chain disruptive processes gives the tech companies and any industry with fast & sequenced launches, the ability to anticipate and change the business, in response to the competitive and business needs. In Apple's case, Phillip Schiller, the current Chief of Marketing, is tasked with the right strategy for brand positioning of new products.

In the hi-tech industry, products such as iPhone have several variants. The market demand fluctuates between variants, and many times, the wrong variant stock is available and there is a shortage in the field. Many companies have worked out an ***Optimal Postponement Strategy*** to maintain the right level of raw material in reserve, to make the components. Network Design ensures that products are available on schedule. So, product planning, competitive pricing, plant location and initial launch are key priorities for the hi-tech products. The challenging supply chain decisions for best market introduction are leveraging partnerships, near shoring or offshoring supply chain, right sizing inventory, optimal postponement strategy, channel distribution planning, capacity planning and supply chain contingency planning, and are the next set of priorities for these hi-tech products. Distribution channels should manage the best tax structure for the decision of where to make for which market.

SUPPLY CHAIN AND PRODUCT STRATEGY PRIORITIES

The first analysis in the hi-tech is to ensure that the desirable features that are expected for the product or service, stand out for the customer. Figure 4.3 is popularly called the QFD form, or quality functional deployment. QFD is the literal translation of the Japanese title, *Hinshitsu Kino Tenkai*. In reality, it is a **Customer Inspired Product Development (CIPD)** process. The real essence of CIPD is a ranking system to identify the key needs of the product and translate them to product and supply chain priorities. CIPD is the technique that gives the guideline to supply chain to prioritize the supply base to enable key partnerships in the assembly and build of the product or service.

Looking at the iPod, Steve Jobs wanted to introduce a product that was a brand driver with easy mobility, high fidelity music and a large personal library. He also planned a disruption of music sales by providing a means for customers to purchase and maintain their own music, with an easy-to-use interface that has been a hallmark of Apple from day one. A visual display provided the interface and ability to view videos as well. These customer requirements are listed on the left side of the table in Figure 4.3. So, the customer requirements for iPod were:

1. Brand driver (Apple wanted each product to be distinct from the others in the marketplace)

2. Mobility

3. High Fidelity music

4. Ability to purchase and store music and videos

5. Large personal library

6. Ease of use

7. Visual Display

Each of these customer requirements were rated against the product spec that Apple had laid out. Apple wanted a small package size and small weight so that the product was easy to carry. The large memory gave the ability to carry a thousand songs in the iPod at a time. The fast processor and output power gave high fidelity of music.

With an adjustable sound and a good video screen the product would have all the features. When Apple rated against the competition, the fast processor, video screen and iTunes library were unique features along with software features such as online playlists. Some tradeoff of features was important, such as a large battery size would add weight but give enough battery life. The correlations were rated as strong positive, positive, none, strong negative and negative, so that the values could be traded off. Using the scores (strong- s :10, medium- m :7, weak-w:4), the product objectives were rated. Apple managed the design, while strategic partners such as Toshiba managed the hardware components. Apple setup strategic partnerships for each element in the component and manufacturing strategy.

New tech is a part of the launch. Each product in the hi-tech is centered around a new feature that is driven to the market, ahead of its availability to the mass market. Apple's identification of this new tech, in this case digital storage of music, was key to the execution of the value proposition. So, in Apple's case the product and supply chain priorities were to start with the launch of the iTunes store ahead of the iPod launch. The iTunes created the right atmosphere for the iPod launch.

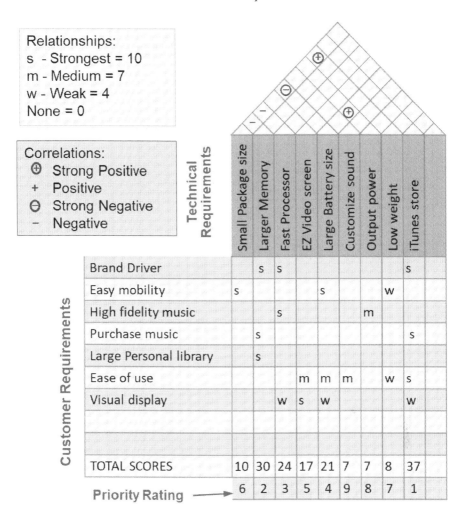

Figure 4.3: QFD form for developing supply chain priorities
The Customer Inspired Product Development Process

INVENTORY PLANNING FOR NEW BUSINESS STRATEGIES

"For a goods and services company, inventory is the lifeblood of the company" – Early 20th century business wisdom.

In any company, day-to-day sales are driven by the available inventory. However, this inventory cost can be a double-edged sword. The availability of inventory gives customers wider choices and flexibility for purchase. Too much inventory, means that money is tied up as working capital and this in turn means less return of investment on the company. Therefore, inventory can be an asset and a liability for the company. The key to optimizing the profitability is the inventory strategy.

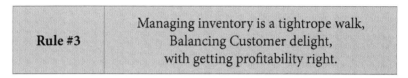

Rule #3	Managing inventory is a tightrope walk, Balancing Customer delight, with getting profitability right.

Before we get into the details of optimal inventory strategy, let's take a quick primer on inventory costs. The cost of inventory relates to the type of inventory. Typical types of inventory are **Cycle Stock**, the inventory that is sold and then replaced by fresh stock, **Safety Stock**, the inventory that is held as buffer so that there is no stock-outs, **Pipeline Stock,** the inventory that is in transit, **Decoupling Stock,** inventory held to balance gap between forecasted demand and incoming supply and held between supplier boundaries, **Seasonal Stock** to manage high selling season, **Obsolete Stock,** where the demand is no more, and **In-transit Stock,** which represents stock in transit to the destination.

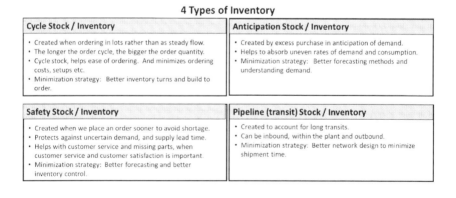

Figure 4.4: Inventory types and Cost Minimization Strategy

The costs associated with these inventories are ordering costs, inventory carrying or warehousing costs and stockout (or lost sales) costs. However, the major cost of inventory is the working capital that is tied up in the inventory itself. The Mom and Pop shop of yesteryears may have carried an average of 90 to 180 days turnover of inventory, compared to their modern-day retail, Walmart that carries about 45 days inventory. So, Walmart needs a quarter of the inventory capital to run a similar operation. The inventory strategy must maintain the minimum stock, across all inventory for a given customer service commitment, planned for the company. Figure 4.4 lists the 4 common types of inventory, and their minimization strategies.

INVENTORY STRATEGY – FROM BULK TO DROP SHIPMENTS

There are case studies, documenting horror stories of inventory problems in the industry. Sometimes during a rapid growth, companies build up excess inventory in anticipation of demand. Cisco had such a situation during the year 2000. Since the router business was skyrocketing on the back of the new growth in home internet and business routers, Cisco built up substantial inventory up to several million dollars. However, the sales did not follow and Cisco had to take a substantial write down of $2.1 billion in its inventory assets. Cisco stock nosedived from a high of $80 to $11.24 in September 2001. The total value lost was more than $140 billion in value, and the firm laid off 8,500 employees. All in all, Cisco wrote off $2.5 billion in inventory. So, the trend nowadays is the lean supply chain. However, as you will see in this section, there is a whole range on either side of lean that needs to be explored for your business strategy.

In deciding your company strategy, it is better that you look through a continuum of inventory management opportunities. The inventory barometer is such a continuum, shown in Figure 4.5. If the customer need is urgent and the loss of sale opportunity cost is extremely high, I recommend that we start with a higher start inventory. On the other end of the spectrum is the drop shipment where all the inventory is held at the supplier's end. Apple excels in this business model and therefore is a market leader in high technology. Apple has perfected the art of sale with its iPhone, while carrying a minimal inventory. Most of the new orders are drop shipped directly from its suppliers. This enables a quick change of product variants and styles, when the market shifts.

Toyota pioneered the concept of Just-in-time and has worked well for many auto industries. It requires a level of trust and continuous demand sharing with all the key suppliers. Consignment is another concept of inventory management.

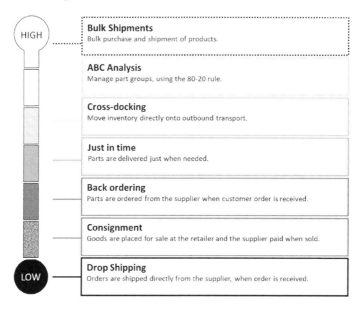

Figure 4.5: Options for Inventory Management in Business

In the supply chain negotiation for Danfoss Power Solutions located in Easley, South Carolina, KP Components, the current supplier, was in the same building. So, the parts availability was executed Just-in-time. However, the new international supplier, Indoshell Ltd, located 8000 miles away. Indoshell provided an attractive product and the author tested and confirmed their product performance and technical compatibility. However, due to the distance, the sticking point was the inventory ownership. The supplier established a new warehouse at the port and a consignment inventory on site to clinch the deal.

The case study of Johnson Controls, in Chapter 3, describes the Just-in-time material handling project. Parts arrive within 2 hours of the build timing. Several of our industrial clients had instituted the Just-in-time process as well. In Asia, Jaguar/Tata and Suzuki have implemented supplier parks, so that the inventory length is minimal from the supplier located down the street in the same industrial park. Several plants in China and India have implemented this strategy.

The typical task in e-commerce retail for inventory shortage is backordering. Amazon maintains a good inventory of its shipment stock. But occasionally, the stock runs out and the new fulfilment date is given to the customer. Automotive companies have thousands of parts per model and have devised the ABC analysis method for managing inventory.

Figure 4.6: Four square sourcing strategy for Strategic to Commodity parts

The ABC plan breaks down the incoming materials into three categories. The high impact, high risk parts are A category, and represent about 20% of the stock, require daily review and maintenance. A dashboard should be created to manage these items. The medium risk/medium impact parts at B, typically represent about 20% and may be analyzed weekly, and low risk/low impact parts such as nuts and bolts, may represent the remaining 60% of the components, may be on automatic reordering process.

Companies, like Walmart have pioneered the cross-docking inventory management. The supplier goods are shipped to a warehouse, staged and then shipped onwards to the final retailer to enable continuous flow of material.

The critical decision for this task is to identify the **Decoupling point**. This location manages the inventory and is the buffer between the demand flow and supply flow. If the decoupling point (where buffer stock is maintained between outgoing demand and incoming supply) is at supplier, backordering, consignment and drop shipment are options. If it is at your company, inventory stock and in-process stock must be managed. Crucial to this activity, is if the supplier is international. Then the network design should account for in-transit stock with port and customs clearance schedules.

INVENTORY STRATEGY – QUICK TURNOVER

Another opportunity for profitability is the business cycle planning. A key supply process in business is the ability to get material in time for your production. While the auto industry can make this happen with the Just-in-time concept, a direct shipment concept of pre-ordering cars is necessary to make the scheme work as a business model.

Dell has instituted this quick turnover of inventory very well. In the best automotive and electronics industries, the inventory turns over about 8 times a year. This KPI means that the inventory held at the manufacturer will satisfy about 1.5 months, (that is in a year, 12 months/8 equals 1.5 months) of inventory available at the supplier at any time. Walmart, one of the most efficient retailers-of-our-time maintains a KPI of 9. However, Dell has a direct shipment business model that enables Dell to maintain an inventory of only 12 days, that is a KPI of 28 and a super-efficient model of business. This translates to a working capital bottom line improvement of three times compared to anyone else in the similar industry, say HP.

The supply chain of this business model with a high inventory turnover, requires key partnerships with suppliers and their willingness to supply material on short notice and on high priority. If the costs of this arrangement can be held to less than savings, the business model will be very effective. Tesla and several low volume car manufacturers have implemented this pattern by creating a demand buzz and a pre-ordering process for low cost and high return. Custom motorcycle companies have also created the same business model and sales on a pre-order basis. This enables a higher margin and a low inventory carrying cost at the dealership and at the manufacturing plant.

INVENTORY STRATEGY – OPTIMAL POSTPONEMENT

One of the crucial strategies that works very well for the hi-tech industry is the *Optimal Postponement Strategy*. Figure 4.7 shows the strategy as a step curve example, that is common in hi-tech and in custom automotive manufacturers. In the US, there may be 3 or 4 variants per model, but in China, there are 8 to 10 variants for each model. So, the curve, shown below tracks the Automotive build plan for an Asian OE.

There are two engine options, 3 transmission options, 3 interior and trim packages and 2 wheel packages. All-in-all there are 10 packages available at the dealer, but 36 variants that can be built to order special packages. So, in a premium SUV, the OE has identified the levels of inventory at each level with the 10 base variants available at the dealer and the remaining 26 variants will be drop shipped (and delivered) to the customer within 14 days. The step chart shows the inventory level at each location, so that the 14 days delivery can be guaranteed.

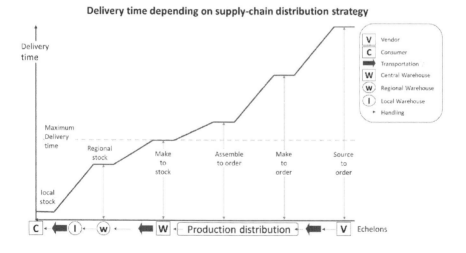

Figure 4.7: Optimal Postponement Strategy

Better management and better business model can utilize these structural inventory strategies into benefits for the organization. Inventory can be saleable goods or any valuable resource management within the company. As we discussed in Chapter 1, inventory in IBM's case was its consultants and their skills. The key takeaway is that inventory is anything, people, product or service enabler, and location planning may be crucial based on support costs. Apple treats its phone features as inventory, and the add/delete feature list, makes the base model or the multiple variations and profitable mix of products.

***

CHAPTER 5

MARKET SEGMENTERS

"Market segmentation is a natural result of the vast differences among people"

– David Norman, American Scientist

In 2003, two engineers, Martin Eberhard and Marc Tarpenning were very frustrated. General Motors had recalled the EV1 electric cars that year and crushed them. The long electric vehicle journey from product development in early 1990s to the testing, evaluation and customer leasing, all had ended in a short time. The future of electric vehicles looked very bleak. So, Martin and Marc started a new company, Tesla, with the prime purpose of making a practical and affordable electric vehicle. They were soon joined by Elon Musk, during the funding rounds. Elon shared their vision for a planet friendly electric car.

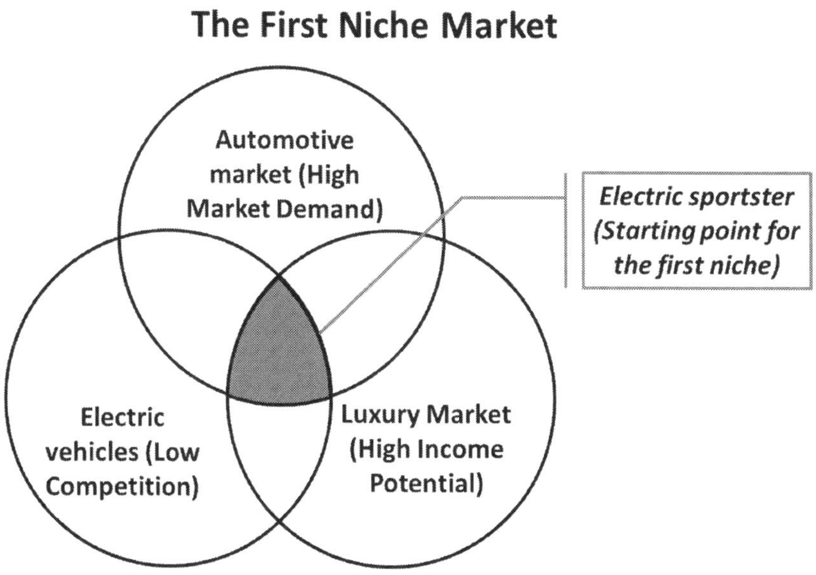

The First Niche Market

Automotive market (High Market Demand)

Electric sportster (Starting point for the first niche)

Electric vehicles (Low Competition)

Luxury Market (High Income Potential)

Figure 5.1: Tesla's first launch plan

Tesla's plan was to start with an electric sportster in the premium segment. The sportster would cost around $100,000 and have an unrivalled performance. It would weigh around 3000 lbs. and have a speed performance of 0-60 mph in under 2 seconds. The car was targeted at early adopters, with a premium price. The product strategy would then go step by step to include lower priced mass market vehicles. The Model S and X would be the second wave, covering the luxury market at a higher volume. The final product plan was the model 3, that would be the ultimate high-volume brand. Tesla had taken the electric vehicle segment, a mono segment, by previous standards and introduced a range of products. The company would offer its powertrains and components to other automakers in the electric market and will get the economies of scale with the combined volume.

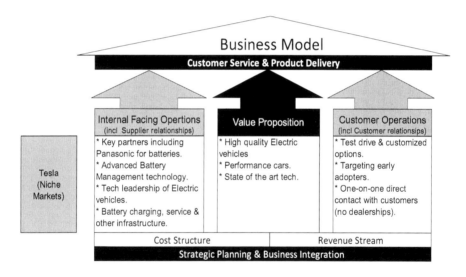

Figure 5.2: Business model of Tesla, a Hyper Segmenter.

The concept of the niche startup to mass branding is not new. In the early 1900s when car market was starting up, Ford was the first mass market brand. Ford made an affordable family car, the model T. Henry Ford in his autobiography, famously wrote, that he will "give customers any color as long as it is black". Ford was successful with the Model T, until General Motors introduced various colors for cars. The "General" ruled the car market in the 1920s when they rewrote the mantra with a car for "every purse, purpose and personality". The niche market of colors marketing had gone mainstream, even though a color vehicle had a higher price than the Model T. Tesla's business model is shown in Figure 5.2.

In a mass market brand, demand variability is a huge concern. In Automotive, any brand sales volume fluctuates from 4 to 15% from period to period[4]; However, the sales of specific options vary as much as 50% over the same period. This provides an ideal segmenting opportunity. Segmenting brands can leverage this opportunity with a dedicated supply chain stream, thereby managing the material flow and the cost to match the demand requirements.

Market research has identified that customer behavior is a truly measurable means of market segment. Customers tend to buy products and services repeatedly, based on a behavior pattern that can be identified. Internet sales companies frequently take advantage of this behavior by targeting ads for similar products, once you have shown interest in an aligned product. You may have searched for organic food restaurants on your phone, and the next day when you log on to your computer, you see an ad for the home delivery of organic foods from a new company. Brand research consultants have identified that the best reproducible segmenting behaviors begins with your previous purchasing habits, followed by your current interests and engagement levels. A listing of the brand segmentation behaviors is shown in Figure 5.3.

Segmentation is all about value efficiency. A true benefit of value efficiency is that the Marketing segmentation should lead to **Supply chain segmentation**. Gartner research, the supply chain analytics firm defines supply chain segmentation[5] as "Designing and operating distinctly different end-to-end value chains (from customers to suppliers) optimized by a combination of unique customer values, product attribute, manufacturing and supply capabilities, and business value considerations". By giving customers more of what they want and less of what they don't want,

[4]Vehicle sales statistical data from www.statista.com. General Motors sales at https://www.statista.com topics/2480/general-motors/

[5]Supply Chain segmentation definition from Gartner. This can be found at https://www.gartner.com/it-glossary/supply-chain-segmentation

efficiency is maximized. This can be done only with a customized supply chain. The bundling and delivery mechanism should be targeted to the delivery needs analysis.

Segmenting Customers

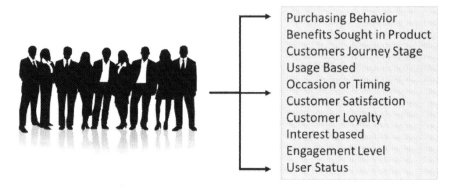

Purchasing Behavior
Benefits Sought in Product
Customers Journey Stage
Usage Based
Occasion or Timing
Customer Satisfaction
Customer Loyalty
Interest based
Engagement Level
User Status

Figure 5.3: The behavior segmentation strategy

Segment Profile for Tesla Customers

General	Demographic

• **Region:** North America, Asia, Europe
• **Location:** Urban & Semi urban (high)
  & Rural (moderate)
• **Age:** 30+
• **Gender:** Male and Female
	• **Occupation:** Working professionals
	  Executives, Senior Managers
	• **Loyalty:** First time, Loyalists

Behavioral	General

• **Benefits sought:** Environmentally
  friendly, Perception of environmentally
  friendly, Status, Life time cost
  effectiveness
• **Personality:** Determined & Ambitious
• **User status:** Potential users, Nonusers
  and first time users
	• **Social class:** Middle class, Upper class
	• **Lifestyle:** Early adopter, aspirational

Figure 5.4: Segmenting customers for Tesla

Rule #4	Segmentation in Customers unlocks value, But Synergy in supply chain adds value

CASE ANALYSIS

Now we will look at a detailed example of how to leverage the segmentation in business, revisiting Happy Singh from Sterling Heights. If you remember Happy Singh, from Chapter 3, was reworking his stamping and fine blanking business. Happy had 5 major customers and a summary of the part numbers and business strategy is shown in Table 5.1 and Table 5.2.

#	Customer	Tier	Part description	Margin	Unique Parts	Logistics type
1	A	Tier 1	Powertrain Components	Excellent	5	DAP
2	B	Tier 2	Vehicle Components	Good	6	DAP
3	C	Tier 1	Refrigerator panels	Low	5	EXW
4	D	Tier 1	Motor covers	Low	4	EXW
5	E	Tier 1	Washer lids	Low	6	EXW
				Total	26	

Table 5.1: Current supply plan with daily changes in delivery

Legend: Logistics includes DAP – Delivered at Place and EXW- Ex works (ready for customer pickup).

In Sterling Heights, Southeast Michigan, Happy was making money on some customers and loosing on some others. One of the main headaches for a one-size-fits-all supply chain is the demand and supply variation. His customer demand ranged from daily & weekly delivery to the production line. Imagine the Supply Chain and Operations (S & Op) planning for this stretch of products. So Happy broke the operations into a series of scope changes for the S & Op. The first question was the division of regular S & Op to three separate streams. He needed a structured breakup of the one size S & Op process to handle multiple streams of demand.

1. Daily S & Op (8:30am daily) priorities:

a. Review demand forecast for all customers.

b. Planning and follow-up for daily deliveries for Just-in-time customers.

c. Planning needs for weekly demand customers.

d. Handling incoming daily supplies and supplier follow-ups.

e. Daily scheduling plans for production.

2. **Weekly S & Op (1pm Wednesday):**

a. Handling suppliers from Central and Mountain time zone.

b. Scheduling of weekly demands.

c. Confirm pickup schedule with the customer.

3. **Monthly S & Op (3pm on First Monday in the month):**

a. Business development plan and acquisition of low volume part development.

b. Planning of filler jobs to manage manpower and machine utilization efficiency.

c. Discuss with Engineering manager on new processes for prototyping requirements as a part of the filler jobs. This was a business development activity.

d. Review all promise dates within 30 days.

e. Work with Boeing (new business development) and West coast suppliers.

COST TO SERVE MODEL FOR SUPPLY CHAIN

The first rule in Segmentation is to identify the right segmentation for each customer. B2B customers may be interested in quality, delivery timing, service level ability to meet variation, scalability etc. in their product delivery. A *Cost to Serve* model can be developed, if the customer priorities can be segmented into value streams. Each valid segment of the model will have a tailor-made agreement to ensure delivery meets the customers expectation on their target priorities.

Rule #5 (by Dr. Philip Kotler)	Segmentation should be measurable, substantial, accessible, differentiable and accountable.

Cost to serve sets up the actions for supplier selection, sourcing, manufacturing plan, inventory buffers, warehousing, shipment methods, fulfillment and promise dates. Multiple supply networks go through the one plant layout. The SMART toolbox for the Market Segmenter is shown in Figure 5.5.

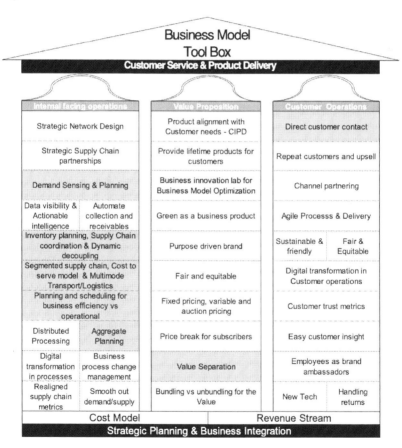

Figure 5.5: The SMART toolbox for Market Segmenters

Automotive Tier I required daily delivery and daily supply since the production schedules change on a daily basis. A local supplier was identified for this raw material. For the appliance market, Happy had the ability to plan the raw material and this came by truck from Illinois. The material supplier was able to give some discount for this material grade requirement. So Happy was able to use the appliance grade alloy steel rather than the automotive grade, for a price savings. So, the ***cost to serve*** per pound of steel was in line with the customer expectation.

Having clearly segmented the customers, our firm advised Happy on the need to set different priorities for the products in the company. Since the demand data was updated daily, the delivery schedules were always under stress. Happy had discussions with the supply chain manager from the automotive and appliance companies to adjust their demand planning needs. There was no way that Happy can meet the demand, with responsiveness and high level of efficiency at the long-term price point agreed with the appliance manufacturer.

After many discussions they agreed to create a decoupling stock at their warehouse and provide a weekly demand forecast. The decoupling demand created a buffer. On the downstream end, Happy was able to switch suppliers who were willing to provide weekly supply from a vendor managed inventory. This way Happy could create a segment for the unpredictable or rapidly changing daily deliveries and balance with the decoupled buffer for the more predictable weekly demand from the second customer. He effectively created different stocking plans. This plan is also called the portfolio approach by some experts.

Secondly, Happy was able to work out the demand signals from the customers. In a weekly demand, Happy used to get calls from customer's buyers two or three times a week asking to revise the ERP demand for that week. This was chaotic and required continuous monitoring. Happy implemented a rush charge for changes to the forecast within the week. This discouraged the changes and made it cost effective for the inventory buffer held at the customer warehouse.

Happy hired a new supply chain manager, with the responsibility for business development and process reinvention. Lessons learned from one customer were implemented for other customers, including a specific process for ordering, fulfillment, inventory and sourcing for each customer. By this process, each demand has a unique service policy, inventory policy, customer replenishment plan and is allocated the appropriate "cost to serve" target. Such a policy needs constant review and automation if there are more than a handful of streams. These are the key ingredients of the *supply chain segmentation.*

Customer	Part description	Material certification	Customer delivery schedule	Logistics type
A	Powertrain Components	Daily	6 days/week	DAP
B	Vehicle Components	Daily	2 days/week	DAP
C	Refrigerator panels	Daily	Weekly	EXW
D	Motor covers	Daily	Weekly	EXW
E	Washer lids	Daily	Bi-weekly	EXW
			Total	26

Table 5.2: The proposed supply chain delivery plan

Rule #6	Global segmenting in supply chain is a gold mine. Market opportunity and target resource use at the same time.

In conclusion, business segmenting is very visible in the new products that are being launched in the disruptive market of today. However, companies are not taking advantage of the full benefits of supply chain segmenting.

***

CHAPTER 6

NEW ECOSYSTEM+ DISRUPTOR

"Developing the new ecosystem is the American Keiretsu"

–Paraphrasing David Burt, author.

Definitions: Keiretsu – A powerful alliance of Japanese businesses often linked by cross-shareholding (Meriam Webster). Also, **Jituan** – A business conglomerate (Chinese online dictionary).

When I (Shawn) landed for my assignment in PATAC, the Pan Asian Technical Center at Shanghai GM in 2006, I was in for a surprise. Shanghai GM (SGM) is a joint venture between SAIC, the Shanghai Automotive Industrial Corporation, China and General Motors, US and is consistently in the top two automotive producers in China. The product portfolio and the technology path at the Chinese joint ventures are somewhat dictated by the foreign partner. However, the suppliers are typically part of a Jituan and hence have a high level of cross breeding in technology and control their own growth path.

The Jituan are connected horizontally and vertically. The horizontal element involves a common ownership, typically by a state entity. There may be two or three suppliers for similar components, each owned by different state entities, involved in a single project. The vertical element is the product flow from raw materials to component assembly and system integration, and it may be through one or more Jituan companies from end to end. This is the key strength of China's auto industry (Ahrens, 2013). China is considered "a workbench of the world[6]" in process technology and cost targets, due to this upstream integration and supplier strength.

---

[6] Total Cost of Global Sourcing in China by Prof. Dr. Michael Eßig, Dr. Andreas Glas, Karl J. Grajczyk, Bundewehr, University of Munich, Supply Chain Management III/2013

Sourcing in China is dictated by the Jituan (pWC, 2008). Many of the world class China suppliers are in Shanghai, Beijing and Guangzhou. They supply SGM and GM, electronic parts, aluminum wheels and interior trim components, such as sun visors, chrome and plastic parts. The sourcing and procurement processes are unique for SGM. The suppliers work with SGM, in the full knowledge that they are competitive and will get the final bid. So, the bid process is non-existent for the Jituan suppliers. Pricing targets ensure the efficiency of the supplier. SGM audits its suppliers in China and elsewhere for quality, process capability, throughput and results.

Rule #7 (From the book, Strategy rules: The Five Timeless lessons from Bill Gates, Andy Grove & Steve Jobs)	Build Ecosystems and Products; Not Just products.

NEW ECOSYSTEM OR AMERICAN KEIRETSU

The big three hi-tech players, Apple, Intel and Microsoft have understood this concept well. The horizontal element of cross ownership is not realistic outside centrally planned economies. But, the vertical element can be a strength in an ecosystem of companies. Apple has understood this element better than anyone else. Enclosed is the Apple's business model in Figure 7.1. While Apple's retail store activities are evident, the details of the Internal Facing Operations and strategy is not in the public domain. So, to fully comprehend the Ecosystem model and its benefits, let us bring in a second example as well. Maruti Suzuki Ltd is the Indian subsidiary of the Japanese company, Suzuki. Suzuki has developed a supplier ecosystem in India that is transparent and offers a great insight to the Ecosystem model.

For an effective Ecosystem supply chain, we need substantial information sharing between the members of the chain. If supply chain can create value and coordinate seamlessly, with flow across the chain and between the supply chain members, then it is a competitive advantage, one that others cannot easily reproduce. This creates a basis for business process to be improved radically. The business model of Maruti Suzuki is shown along with Apple's iPhone in Figure 6.1. The supply chain tool box for the Ecosystem model is shown in Figure 6.2.

In 1981, the Government of India invited Suzuki, the Japanese motorcycle and small vehicle manufacturer to setup an automotive manufacturing venture, first as a partner, then later as a stand alone public company. In the 80s, Suzuki was the leader in small vehicles in Japan but has now become the volume leader in India and a leading & efficient contract manufacturer for Toyota and Nissan brands, with small-car sales in Europe, Africa and US markets.

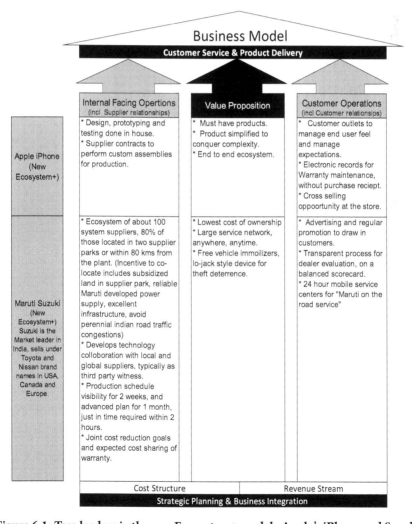

Figure 6.1: Two leaders in the new Ecosystem+ model - Apple's iPhone and Suzuki

In contrast to Suzuki's popular motorcycle market worldwide, Suzuki started with small cars and has moved to bigger vehicles and SUVs. With the head start over the competition, Jaguar/Tata and Hyundai, Suzuki has a solid lead with nearly half the market. To start things off, Suzuki setup a supplier park in Gurgoan, near New Delhi (Julka, 2014). Here the suppliers were encouraged to setup their manufacturing base. These are the first tools in creating the Ecosystem, **Supply Chain Partnerships** and **Supplier Network Design**. Suzuki enables this network concept by choosing the most capable and willing partners. The supplier selection tasks may be through audits, internal assessments, or through extensive questionnaires. The suppliers are then ranked for their ability to contribute in the Ecosystem. (for more details on supplier ranking, see Figure 12.4). Suzuki then negotiates with each potential supplier to establish their value and create a contract to bring them in to the Ecosystem.

The supply chain agreements are detailed to include data sharing, level of service required and the cost-benefit model with the potential upside revenue sharing and downside warranty cost sharing with each supplier. Each supplier goes through a training process and may be assigned a small revenue project, to establish the track record. Key customer metrics of risk, cost, quality and delivery management are agreed in the contract. The returns are calculated by customer metrics, such as ROCCE - Return On Common Capital Employed and DOTIF - Delivered On Time In Full.

There are several working elements in the supply chain partnerships. Suzuki has introduced several plans to streamline its supply chain. The company reduced its Tier 1 suppliers from 370, in the 2000s to about 100 now.

Cost sharing is also implemented with the supplier. The material cost to net sales reduced from 90% in 2000-2001 to 79% in 2008-09 and substantially better today. No Ecosystem can perform without the efficient sharing of information between the Ecosystem partners. The key enabler is **data visibility** and transparency (CIO team, 2009). Cost drivers in design are constantly revised based on supplier processes. The Ecosystem model is directly opposed to the process in other OE competitors.

A typical process in other OEs include a bidding process, where the engineering team works with multiple suppliers. The final sourcing award is done after the design is completed at each supplier. There is a tight working relationship between R&D, Purchasing, Component development, Quality, Master Scheduling and Output planning. Suzuki ensures that its parts are delivered Just-in-time, with almost 80% of the suppliers located within the supplier park or within 80 miles of the production facility.

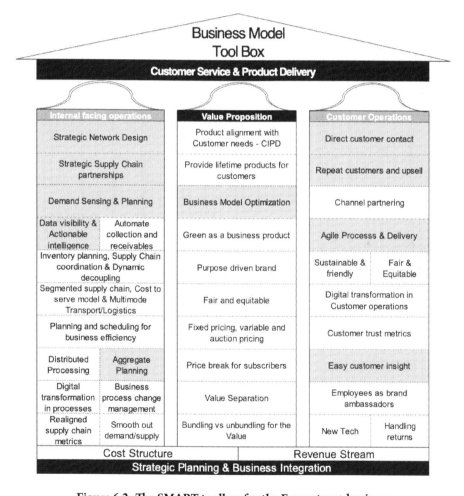

Figure 6.2: The SMART toolbox for the Ecosystem+ business

One key requirement for each supplier in the Ecosystem is to invest in capability upgrades of EDI, the electronic data interchange system for data transfer across the Ecosystem. A supply chain council led by the OE supply chain manager regularly reviews the performance of each supplier and communicates with the stake holders.

The pricing and features of all Suzuki's offerings have been an irresistible combination for market sales. Suzuki's launch of the Grand Vitara had 100,000 units of preordered cars. Since the production was scheduled after preorders, **demand sensing** was an easy result. Parts are delivered by the supplier within 2 hours of production. Suzuki has 100 tier-1 suppliers, and each is a system aggregator. **Aggregate planning** creates a smoothening of demand.

A similar market pull, such as the Grand Vitara was seen in each of Apple's iPhone launches. Preorders were drop shipped from the supplier directly to the end customer, creating an **agile delivery process**. Aggregate planning is done through optimal postponement, where the common parts for multiple variants are kept in stock, until the order. The parts are then assembled into the final product, so there is no work in progress inventory mismatch to the demand. Apple has created a unique Ecosystem, by supplier selection and cross training and cross sharing information across suppliers.

Apple has extended the Ecosystem concept to include the customer interface. Retail stores manage the customer experience, with **direct customer contact**. Each store has the ability to collect customer feedback, an essential ingredient for growing the business. Retail stores may do a soft sell, suggesting an upgrade when the current product is close to end of life.

The following are the steps involved in an Ecosystem selection process.

CHOOSE THE RIGHT ECOSYSTEM PARTNERS

In 2007, Suzuki entered into a partnership with Magneti Marelli from Italy to localize AMT transmission manufacturing in India. Similarly, Suzuki entered into a partnership with Futuba Industrial Co. Ltd from Japan, to manufacture exhaust systems in India. Suzuki has joint ventures with a strategic equity stake with 19 of the 246 tier-1 and tier-2 suppliers and has decision rights production and quality fulfilment of parts (Julka, 2014).

The first step in building any supply chain ecosystem is to identify the in-house and the partnership needs of the organization. Once the planning is complete, a suitable partner can be selected for the fit strategy. In supply chain partnerships, businesses manage their vertical relationship and reduce the business risk through commitments. This vertical relationship works in the channel partnership as well, minimizing the risk of product availability at the customer end.

Other businesses may setup an intersectional partnership. For example, many organizations have joined together to establish the gear consortium at Ohio State University and the driverless car testing site at the University of Michigan. This partnership has the specific purpose of technology as a driver for their charter. The joint venture is the structure preferred by many companies, when they setup a facility at a new international location. The partners bring the technology knowledge and the local business/cultural knowledge to make the partnership work together.

Companies may also take equity stake in each other to cement their relationship. Tractors and Farm Equipments Ltd, located in Chennai, India, is the world's third largest volume manufacturer for tractors and has a relationship with AGCO Manufacturing Company, Duluth, Georgia, US, for technology tie-up as an equity partner. Here AGCO brings technology R&D and TAFE brings marketing clout. Strategic partnerships have a chartered purpose and the agreed access to decision making. Cobranding, for a joint benefit in branded sales and development partnerships, for ensuring partner companies pool resources for new development, are also common.

A supply chain Ecosystem with platforms of products will ensure a collective synergy in product launch and supply chain strengths of independent suppliers, to get great products and services to the market. As has been demonstrated by Apple, many Chinese companies and Suzuki in India, the Ecosystem model offers the best competitive edge in the marketplace.

Choosing the right Ecosystem partner is the key in this business model.

***

Chapter 7

On Demand disruptor

".... [W]inning in today's marketplace requires an understanding that the supply-driven business models of the past will not keep pace with the fundamental changes in our global economy and its digitally enabled consumer"

- Jack Welch.

Imagine that you are a junior lawyer, a Gen Y, and you have recently started work in a city, like Chicago. Living downtown in Chicago, it is hard to get around in your own car. Driving and parking downtown are challenging. If you prefer a covered carport in your condo complex, it is available for purchase at a substantial cost with financing through a bank mortgage. It is a weekday morning and you are taking Lyft to work, and you arrive at 9am. During the drive, you listen to your podcast subscription at genylawyers.com and learn about real estate trends in Chicago. Parking at work is subsidized, but still costs about $300 per month. You are happy to skip that expense, along with car payments, maintenance, taxes, titles, etc.

You walk up to your office from the lobby and your work day begins. The law firm had launched a new app the previous month for pay as-you-go legal services. Today, you have 4 new clients that each have 20 minutes of free consultation. Client calls are now routed through an intelligent AI server, that identifies the client's legal issues and a list of similar cases as precedents. You review the precedents and prepare to discuss the cases with them. Your back-office staff - secretary, paralegal etc., that used to support your work has gone down from the one on one ratio, to one staff for about 8 lawyers.

Lunch is delivered through Uber eats. You like Uber eats, since the delivery times are managed more accurately than the local restaurant delivery vans. While eating your lunch, you decide to do your personal planning for the weekend. Next week, your parents are coming, to spend a few days with you. They will enjoy the change of scene with a downtown stay, coming in from Memphis, TN. They may want to visit friends on the west side suburbs for an evening dinner. So, you get them a Zipcar rental as well. You order groceries through Instacart, and setup the Doordash app on the iPad, so that they can order food. You suddenly realize that 2 extra days stay with your parents, will be hard. So, you jump on Airbnb app and organize a two day stay for them at the Wisconsin Lake Villas.

Your kid brother is going to the prom next weekend and had called you during the weekend to help him with some planning and expenses. You decide that you are going to get him a Tux rental and a limo service. So, you go to Blacktux.com & blacklane.com and complete the transactions. You finish all the app booking - lunch, grocery, stay, tux and limo, in under one hour. Now, you must meet the next client.

The on-demand delivery windows for these applications are getting shorter and shorter. Amazon has the one day and same day deliveries available in many cities across the US. Recently, Amazon has begun experimenting with the Amazon flex that will deliver in one hour. Amazon flex is in beta test, using the driver app to get independent drivers to deliver packages. Drivers are paid $18 to $25 per hour to use their own vehicle to deliver packages in a given sector. The app tracks drivers through the phone GPS, to ensure delivery time and accuracy.

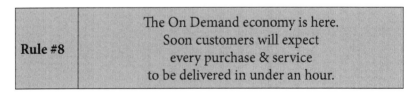

Rule #8	The On Demand economy is here. Soon customers will expect every purchase & service to be delivered in under an hour.

The pace of growth of the on-demand economy is through the rapid adoption by the tech companies. On the other side, for example, an average American uses a car for about 50 min in a day, according to AAA. The cost and management of a vehicle as a resource for less than 5% usage, compared to the 95% of the idle time is considered as a no go, especially by the Gen Y millennials. By trading the ownership for an access to a car when needed, has given rise to such services as Lyft and Uber. Similarly, Airbnb has capitalized on rooms available at private homes. The basic user principle is that it is better to rent and fill the part time need than to own it. Now let's look at the business model for Hilti Tools, that has scaled its operations to support its new on-demand business.

HILTI ON-DEMAND TOOL BUSINESS

Hilti is a Lichtenstein based, European multinational tool manufacturer, that manufactures tools and products for the construction, building maintenance, energy and manufacturing industries. While Hilti makes many power tools for the consumer market, it is very popular in the commercial market for its fire protection, measuring tools, specialty drills etc. Hilti has had many years of experience renting out tools through the Home Depot tool rentals business segment. Many tools made by Hilti are a must have for construction, and now, Hilti has developed an on-demand tooling rental service that is a disruptor in the tool sales business.

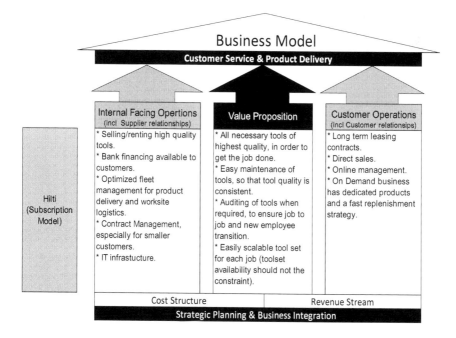

Figure 7.1: Hilti's On Demand business model (Hilti, 2019)

In construction and machinery trades in the US, tooling maintenance is a hazzle. If your workforce is constantly changing, maintaining a common set of tools is very difficult. So, Hilti has developed an effective tooling demand service. Hilti's on-demand business has three levels. The first level includes Tool Fleet Management, where Hilti offers tools that the customer uses consistently for long term use, at the lowest cost, with tax deductible monthly billing and auditing options when customer jobs and personnel change over. The second level is Tools on Demand, for seasonal tools in fleet management. The third level is the tooling rental program for occasional use, such as was done through Home Depot before. Figure 8.1. shows the business model for Hilti.

SCALABILITY IN ON-DEMAND BUSINESS

The SMART toolbox for the On-Demand economy is shown in Figure 7.2. The main supply chain challenge for the On-Demand economy is *scalability and the planning and scheduling for business efficiency* instead of operational efficiency. In construction trades, the contractor may be at a large house construction for the first project, moving to a commercial strip mall development, followed by a regular mall development. The constant constraint for this switch-up is the toolset required, since the workmen change with each project.

In most firms, the key metric for the internal operation is the throughput for the time period. This maximizes the operational efficiency and is a good standalone metric for the traditional business models of the 20th century. However, if the business is planning for the On-Demand economy, throughput efficiency is not the only metric and this metric should be incorporated into a complete balanced set of *customer centric metrics*. The operation should be able to scale up and down to accommodate the growth in On-Demand volumes. Balancing the operational and business efficiency is a key task. The migration path from the traditional business model to the On-Demand business model requires iterative cycles of growth. In the first iteration, companies typically provide additional inventory buffer to handle the changes in On-Demand needs. The next step in the evolution is to simplify the operational process so that the products or service can be produced with less operational overheads. One common method that companies such as Hilti have been able to use for this task, is distributed processing. Agile product fulfillment and replenishment strategy are customer metrics for Hilti.

Scalability and distributed processing have been an age-old concept in IT but is increasingly a new and important concept in On-Demand services. Scalability is the system ability of the supply chain network and every demand process to accommodate growth in demand. On-Demand services require an assured customer service level and the availability of necessary resources for the On-Demand needs within the customer's expectations. For instance, we discussed the case of TVS 99 in Chapter 2, where the scooter manufacturer decided to offer 99 colors on its small scooter lines. So, Asian paints as the strategic supply partner, installed On-Demand facilities in every metro area, to turnaround finished scooters in 24 hours in metros and in 48 hours at a given radius around the metro. **Distributed processing** gives the opportunity to assemble the final product at the customer site and achieve agility.

Scalability planning is a business decision and value-adds but should maintain the business cost structure and manage the load. A contribution margin must be maintained with the resource addition and deletion.

Contribution margin = Revenue - Variable cost.

So, if the pricing plan is independent of volume, then the variable cost must be maintained independent of the volume. In volume scaling, many similar parallel processes are added when the load is increased, so the customer deliveries are maintained at the service level. In throughput or vertical scaling, a new feature is added to the product with a new supply chain loop. This increases the value chain and the revenue. However, a fully vertical scalable supply chain does not compromise the customer delivery commitments. In the introduction of TVS99 is a vertical scalability, that created a new feature on the product. The following supply chain elements are essential for the On-Demand business model:

1. Strategic network planning & demand driven planning.

2. Digital transformation with seamless integration (See Chapter 8).

3. Supply chain with rapid scalability
   a. Plan for continuous growth.
   b. Plan for adaptive and agile supply chain.

4. Customer service actions – very similar to Ecosystem model at Apple's stores
   a. Direct customer contact & up-sell potential with customers.
   b. Agile delivery option.

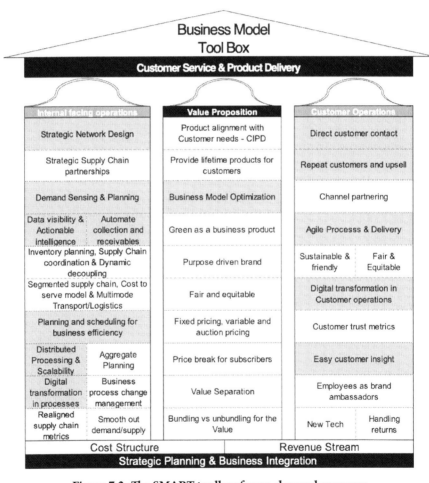

Figure 7.2: The SMART toolbox for on-demand economy

In startups, on-demand app models are very popular due to the ease of scalability. However, with proper management of supply chain, hardware can be the success story, with ramp up and managed supply chain. No wonder, Steve Jobs brought in Tim Cook, the supply chain expert, to relaunch apple in 2005.

Rule #9	In Startups, "Hardware may be hard" But if supply chain is scalable, then progress is unmistakable

Small business example of Scalability

Another approach to scalability is to have a limited base process capability in-house, called creative outsourcing or backup outsourcing. When there is a spike in demand, some external sources can be brought into play. A prime example of this action is in IT. In Cloud services, additional servers can be brought online to handle unusual load.

In small business, this scalability concept has worked well. Saline is an affluent but semi-rural township near Ann Arbor, Michigan. In Saline, the utility company was having high breakdowns of the utility trucks during heavy snow days, with the trucks getting stuck off road or in dirt roads. So the utility company contacted my client, a large towing company in neighboring Ypsilanti, to arrange towing services as a backup for winter times. The client guarantee was that the Utility truck will be picked up within one hour with a penalty fee for missing the hour timeline. So, the towing service created a downstream contract with neighboring areas, Ypsilanti, Ann Arbor and Canton, for priority service when its own trucks were unavailable during heavy snow days.

This was a premium service for twice the cost as normal service but gave high priority for Utility SOS calls from Saline.

***

CHAPTER 8

THE NEW MARKETPLACE

"My job is making money, helping other people make money."

–Jack Ma on Collective entrepreneurship.

I n the 1990s, China was a traditional business market, with all business done face to face. Known as "Guanxi", this face to face culture, required a long-haul act of trust building in business, before sales would follow. In that market, a young entrepreneur, Jack Ma saw the value of the up and coming internet technology and launched the B2C retail company, Alibaba. Fast forward to today, Alibaba is one of the top three tech companies in China and is credited with opening the Chinese product market to the world. Today, Alibaba accounts for half of the package traffic in China.

Alibaba's business value is the ability to connect small and large sellers to their markets around the world. Jack has created two virtual malls - Taoboa for non-branded products and Tmall for branded products. Taoboa and Tmall are the largest retailers in China. With 80% e-commerce penetration in metros and 47% across the country, China is expected to skip the brick and mortar store investment and go to directly to e-tailing.

The new marketplace business model is very simple. It is a two-sided model, bringing the sellers and buyers together in one virtual location. Alibaba's expertise is in creating the platform and developing the marketplace. This new marketplace is also called "joint entrepreneurship," where Alibaba has created a loyal band of co-entrepreneurs, who have cascaded their capability using the platform. Airbnb has a similar business model, bringing house owners and renters together on an online marketplace. In a crowded marketplace, Airbnb curates each listing providing accurate descriptions of the accommodations and provides homeowner's insurance to protect against damage during the stay. Figure 8.1 shows Airbnb and Alibaba business model structures.

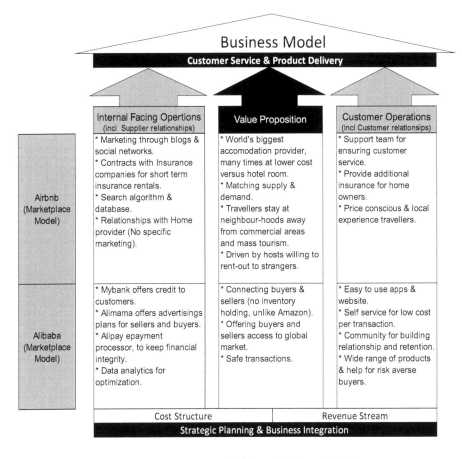

Figure 8.1: Business model for Airbnb and Alibaba
(Airbnb.com, 2018) & (Alibaba.com, 2018)

Other companies have created variants of this model with auction pricing, such as in Priceline.com with bidding for hotel accommodations and Ebay with auction sales. Amazon has added its own line of products and Amazon Prime is another variant with a subscription loyalty service and unique features. Each variant addition strengthens the business model, thereby locking out potential competition and giving the incumbent an advantage.

The main enabler for this strategy is the data access & continued visibility of the marketplace to the potential customers. In the traditional application of a dual sided business, such as ads in the newspaper, the print media was the platform connecting the advertisers and the potential buyers. With internet database, the data can always be visible, 24x7 to the customers, and is actionable, for order taking, delivery tracking etc. The SMART toolbox structure for the New Marketplace model is shown in Figure 8.2.

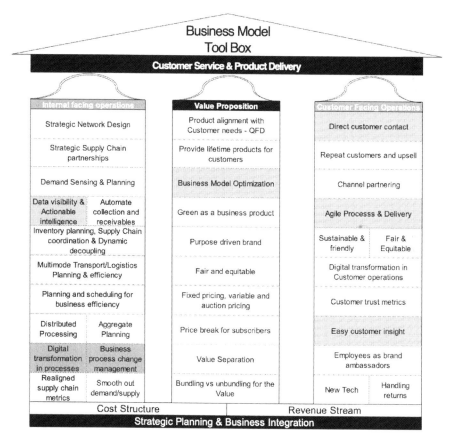

Figure 8.2: The SMART toolbox for the
New Marketplace business

The key supply chain activity is the digital transformation of the business. A gap coverage strategy needs to be established for a good digital transformation. Let's look in detail at the digital transformation strategy.

An ideal representation of the digital transformation is the future bridge strategy, shown in Figure 8.3. The bridge has building blocks to get from the past to the future. The building blocks establish the current strategy and how the transition will ensure the digital future.

In any project, the first step is to identify the value proposition plan, and the gaps in information, data, technology and processes. Since Airbnb and Alibaba's transformation process is not documented, let's discuss this with a small business example where the author and his team were involved.

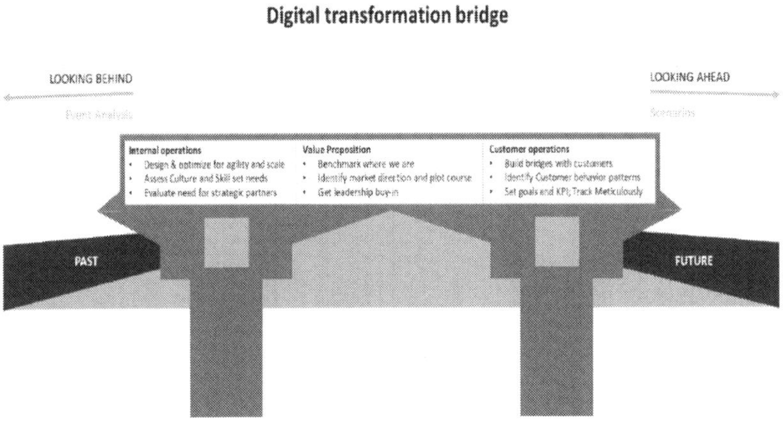

Digital transformation bridge

Figure 8.3: Bridge strategy for Digital transformation

CASE ANALYSIS – THE LANSING STORAGE WARS

In the early 2000s, the self-storage companies in Lansing had a dilemma. Lansing is the industrial city in mid-Michigan, with many auto and supplier plants. Since the city was in a flux, there were several rented units which were going unpaid. Many of the self-storage companies had less than 100 units, losing 1 or 2 units every month made it difficult to collect. Many larger storage companies with higher default units, could hold an auction of repossessed material with a substantial audience bidding for miscellaneous items. Income from these sales, partially offset the losses from the unpaid units.

Rule #10	Digital transformation is creating "the strategy map for the process gaps"

The Lansing area storage companies decided to join forces to auction the material together. This required the identification of the material, inventorying the contents, generating a buzz for bringing in potential bidders, transporting the material to a common location and holding an auction. Some of the high value items could be pre-bid and sold at the storage company, if it is valued and identified on an internet database. The storage companies contacted CFG for advice. With the support of a local consignment store manager, to value and market these materials, a website was created with database of material that was being sold that month. If the customers bid within 10% of the estimated value, then the item was sold before the auction. The remaining items were auctioned every 3rd Saturday of the month. The storage teams agreed on a clear cost-benefit plan. The annual recovery was 92% of the unpaid dues, compared to prior benchmarks, with 52% returns from the larger sales and less than 20% for the smaller sales.

The purpose of digital transformation is to convert the old-style spreadsheet based information into an easily actionable insights and next steps.

	Process vertical	Description	Current state	Future state
1	Value Proposition	Material availabilty	Unknown until date of auction	Useful material bargain prices
2	Value Proposition	Easy bidding	Open auction	Open auction and internet preauction
3	Value Proposition	Easy access to review material	No prior visibility	If bid deposit, preview and sale before auction.
4	Customer Operation	Easy payment	Cash payment	Cash and online credit payment
5	Customer Operation	Auction and customer care manager	On the day of auction	Internet based all month, on-site auction day
6	Internal Operation	Inventory database	Spreadsheet on auction day	Database entry on 2nd Monday of every month
7	Internal Operation	Website support and data entry	None	External company at $100 per month.

Table 8.1: Digital future strategy for Lansing Storage Wars

One of the troubles of scalability is the quick access to additional servers. Recently, Amazon Web Services (AWS) has started a subscription service, offering access to its servers, with software support. This B2B service is very popular around the world. Some of the large trucking companies have decided for fleet tracking, AWS is a scalable need based on the number of trucks out on service at any given time. Many of the world's biggest tech based companies, such as Netflix, Airbnb, Pinterest, Adobe and Citrix, use the Amazon web services for their scalable cloud computing and storage needs.

Besides the digital transformation, the other tools (Figure 8.2) in the toolbox have been covered in the previous models and they apply equally to the new marketplace. Many companies have installed an internet database for their scrap and other materials to find suitable buyers. With minimal investment, other than IT and support service, the new marketplace will prove a good addition to any other existing business model.

***

CHAPTER 9

THE SUBSCRIPTION BUSINESS MODEL

"In all my years, I don't remember anything that has been as successful at getting customer to ship in new product lines"

–**Robbie Schwitzer,** VP on Amazon Prime subscription service.

In 1997, Reed Hastings was returning home from the Blockbuster video store. Blockbuster, the popular video store at that time was the undisputed king of video rentals with more than 6000 stores in its heyday. Blockbuster believed in a strict penalty fee for late returns. Customers would miss returning the video after watching a home movie one weekend, realizing the mistake much later. The store manager in Farmington Hills, Michigan confessed that his revenue collection was a third more due to the late fees on some months.

That day, Reed Hastings was charged $40 in penalty fees for a single video due to late fees. Frustrated with the late fees, Reed decided he wanted to create a competing model. The new movie format, DVDs had just come out a short while ago. It was easier to rent out the DVDs by mail rather than through brick and mortar stores across the country. Along with the innovation of mail order shipping DVDs, he chose the subscription model with options of either one or two DVDs rented out at a time. There would be no late fees. The low monthly subscription cost, and no late fees was attractive for many customers and Netflix subscription business was born. Figure 9.1 shows the Netflix subscription model.

Now, subscription is not a new business model. Many companies and organizations such as trade unions and clubs, charge membership fees. Businesses such as mail order sales, cable television, satellite radio, and cell phone operators have monthly subscription fees. Nowadays, the Dollar Shave Club and Birchbox have such subscription delivery services as well.

The subscription prospect is a sales blessing for the business. In any business, the most difficult task for the CEO is to manage sales month after month. New customer acquisition is a constant task. However, in a subscription business, you have a continuous stream of committed customers. The reduced fluctuations enable a better predictability and a steady Internal Facing Operation for the company.

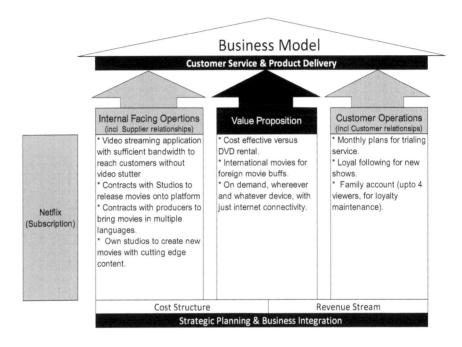

Figure 9.1: Netflix's subscription business model (Netflix.com, 2017)

SMART TOOLBOX FOR SUBSCRIPTION MODEL

The SMART supply chain tool box, Figure 9.2, shows the specific enabling strategies that will empower the subscription business. Let's look at the subscription model, from a small business example.

In the winter of 2006, Tom Banks bought a large gas station in Munro, Michigan, just off the I-75 interstate. There were several other gas stations nearby, and each station was competing for the highway traffic as well as the local travelers that drove to Detroit for work every day. The station sold about 60,000 gallons of gasoline and made an additional store sale of around $40,000 per month. The question was, how do you build loyalty in a fiercely competitive market, so that you can grow the business and have repeat customers at the store.

Tom was able to diversify the store merchandise with some magazine racks, electronic gadgets for the highway travelers and other options. However, the store sales volume was unchanged. In kicking around the loyalty ideas, we decided that Tom can introduce a coffee of the month club. Coffee was a popular sales item, priced at $1 per cup. However, if coffee club was introduced for those regulars willing to purchase a month of coffee, Tom could throw in a coffee mug as well. So, Tom printed out a loyalty card for 30 days. Anyone purchasing the mug for $20, would get 30 days of free refills, with sundry purchase.

Tom generated about 200 customers the first month, and in the next few months when he sold Red wings Stanley cup memorabilia mug, he reached 1000 customers. After the struggle in the first year, Tom did not expect a sudden success of this strategy. Each customer would spend an additional store purchase every time, offering the ability to **repeat customers and upsell**. In a year after the coffee club and free car wash introduction, the store sales rose to 70k gallons and $60k in store, that is 150% revenue increase from the year before.

The losses from the coffee revenue were offset by the new volume of sales from this subscription. Later in the year, he installed a machine that automatically renewed the coffee subscription every month for the customers who sign up. This is **the provision of the lifetime products to the customer**. His neighboring gas stations assumed that it was a money loser and did not follow suit. By the time, the word got around, Tom had built a loyal following, introduced exotic coffees, upgraded his store to include a Subway and sealed the market. In two years, Tom doubled the value of the business from $800k to $1.6 million.

Rule #11	Subscription business is the prescription for steady revenue.

The concept of subscription is used in many industries. Amazon gives a discount for regular deliveries of some staple items, such as detergents. In another example, in the flower sales business, it is a boom or bust, depending on special holidays where flowers are sort after. But H.Bloom, a subscription based company, provides weekly bouquets to hotels for $29. So, in a steady stream the company makes $1508 per customer per year.

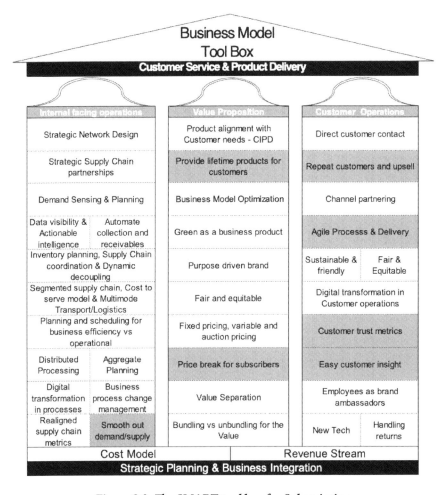

Figure 9.2: The SMART tool box for Subscription

A high percentage of businesses that are switching their models, are now opting for the subscription model. The benefits for the switch over are rather obvious. The prime purpose of the subscription model is to **smooth-out demand.**

The greatest single improvement in the business is that many of the business functions have now become automatic. In dealing with customers, the main issues with the business is the collections after service. In the subscription business, since a small amount is paid monthly, it is typically on a credit card payment schedule. This automates the payment process and eliminates the need for collection and accounting staff. The product or service demand is known for the next sales period. So, it is easier to schedule the service without any loss of inventory due to the smoothness of the demand.

The value proposition to the customer is also clearly visible. Customers purchase on a regular basis, and the price break they get for this repeated purchase is an attractive option for continued sales. Companies have direct access to the customers due to their regular contact. So, companies can develop insights to the customers' needs and wants. Normally this level of insight will require big data analysis and in the case of small business, a third-party specialist to interpret the results. The process of delivery can be agile and scored against **customer trust metrics**. For instance, our home cleaning is done by *twomaidsandamop.com*. The maids do not get paid, unless the customer gives the best review for the cleaning. Such a review will provide access to **easy customer insights**.

Overall, we have found that the subscription model is the easiest to implement from the business capability point of view.

***

CHAPTER 10

TEACH AN ELEPHANT TO DANCE

"The traditional companies have innovated top-down. The new disruptors at 'hackathons', are innovating through open collaboration. To them, you are collateral damage"

–Author unknown

THE GENERAL GETS TO DANCE

General Motors was the undisputed king of the American automobile from the 1920s to the 1980s. In the following decades, with the entry of Toyota, Honda and Hyundai, the competition was fierce and the face of American automobile had changed. But change within the company was slow in coming. I remember on one of my first projects, I had to wait days for the shop floor data to be signed off by the floor supervisor to publish quality data from the floor. At GM-Nummi, GM's collaboration with Toyota, things were very different. The process flow ensured that current data was displayed on the Kanban board and the problem-solving team was driving the next day's production quality.

It was evident in the early 2000s that Toyota or VW will soon surpass GM in volume leadership, but GM was not nimble in product introductions and quality target improvements, two key metrics of growth in the automotive market. New product features such as lane keeper warning, automatic braking and blind spot monitoring, that were first conceptualized by the General were introduced faster by the competition. GM's pace was improving but not as fast as the competition. The final straw that broke the camel's back was the eventual bankruptcy of GM in 2008. GM laid off thousands, closed plants but is now in its current incarnation, nimbler than ever before in its history.

Now the story of GM may be a decade old but is played true in some form or the other in many large corporations. Like the classic allegory, where the frog is being boiled, the gradual rise in the temperature does not cause the frog to jump out, and in the case of corporations that do not change course could stall the company. Whether it was GM in the early 2000s, Toys R Us in 2017 or Sears in 2019, the story is the same. In the grand old scheme, Toys R Us and Sears did not have the government support that General had.

In any product cycle, at maturity there is limited room to grow. Organizations that have committed many resources to the current product, must reevaluate their strategy to be able to reinvent themselves in the next cycle. A business innovation lab is an ideal evaluation tool for this change. Statistics show that the organizations that hit the stall points of growth have only about a 10% chance of reinvention[7]. Time is the critical essence in the process.

ELEPHANT DANCE LESSONS

In 2007, before the GM bankruptcy, GM had setup several initiatives to change course for the company. Rick Wagoner, the Chairman and CEO addressed my team for one such initiative, GoFast that was instrumental in creating a faster decision process. He described the company as a large ship that needed many tugboats to change direction. GoFast was the initiative with external coaches imbedded in business functions to drive quick decision making. In many ways, GoFast was like the job of an elephant trainer, a Mahout.

Many companies take radical steps to change course and culture. Unilever purchased the Dollar Shave Club for one billion dollars to learn the new direct to customer business model, integrate a new subscription business process and to enter the shaving blades market. Proctor & Gamble is the market leader with its Gillette brand in that market. P&G and Unilever are tough competitors but have a similar business model. Figure 10.1 shows the business model details for the two companies.

---

[7] HBR Review, March 2008, "When growth stalls".

Now, let's understand the planning and synergy required for this business model change. In any product life cycle, the customer population willing to adopt this product innovation from early birds (Early Adopters) to late comers (Laggards), is shown by the bell curve in Figure 10.2. The cumulative accumulation of customers committed to the same product is shown by the dashed lines in the same figure.

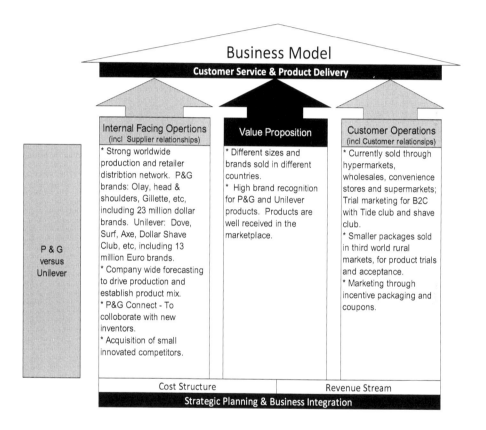

Figure 10.1: Business model at Consumer goods leaders

In the 20th Century, product changeover was an occasional incidence and most companies had time to process a change, whether it is a product refresh or a replacement product. However, in the current times, product cycles are quick and any delay in a replacement product or a missed product feature can spell doom for the company.

Take for instance the automotive marketplace in India. Companies are investing heavily in engine and driveline improvements to meet stricter emissions, while the country jumps from level 4 to level 6 of Corporate Average Fuel Economy (CAFÉ) and tailpipe emission (CARB) standards, all in one jump. China and India, in their eagerness to meet the Paris accord, have shortened the changeover from ten years to five years for this change. Despite this cost burden for the new engine technologies, the local market in China and India is exploding with new products and the companies have found unique ways to reduce the cost impact to the customer. Companies can grow or stall, if they miss the window of change.

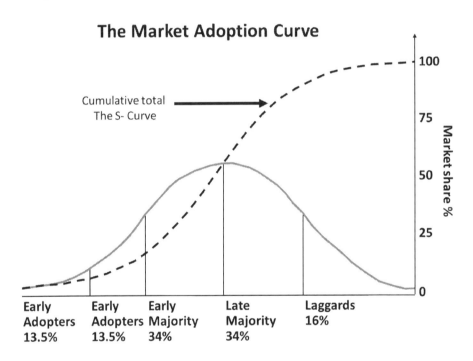

Figure 10.2: Product life cycle, S-Curve

For a smooth execution of the company, the sales structure must transition from the market S-curve of one product to the next product in smooth succession. The task is to ramp up the next business, while the previous business is slowing down. This is called spring boarding the S-Curve and is shown in Figure 10.3.

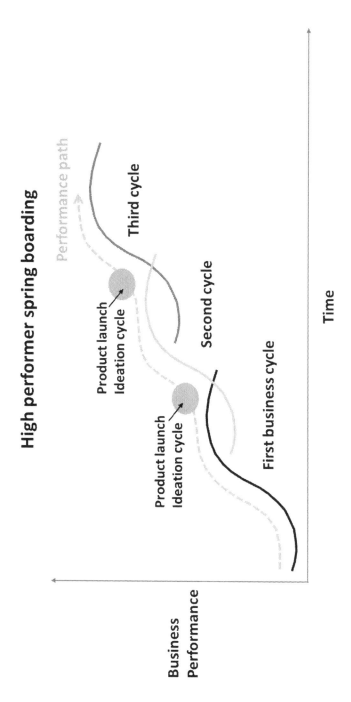

Figure 10.3: Spring boarding the S-Curve (Nunes, 2011)

The figure shows a sequence of S-Curves in quick succession. High performers create a path that effectively goes from the beginning of one product, to a mix of two products, one mature and other just launching. By the time the first product has reached end of life, the company is well established in the next product. And the sequence repeats.

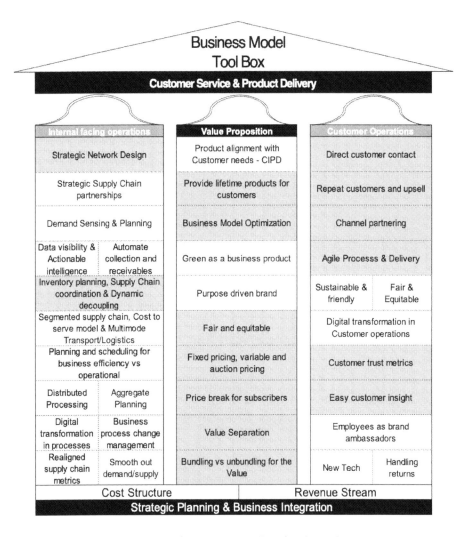

Figure 10.4: The SMART toolbox for the Mahout

A Small business example

Let's look at this small business perspective. Take for instance, Mr B's bar and grill that opened in Farmington Hills, at a former Italian restaurant location. The new bar has a business model where customers have a chance to come in to decompress after work, a week day after work bar.

After the bar opened, we discussed with them that there were many former patrons, who came during the remodeling and probably will come again looking for the convenience of the Sunday brunch. So, the owners decided to open the side door to the private dining room for the Sunday crowd. Mr. B's retained the old cook from the prior restaurant to cater the home cooked meal, Italian style.

The bar atmosphere cleaned up every Sunday for a nice Sunday brunch, in a well-lit private party room.

The Corporation that is considering a serious change has to establish a strong disruptor model, should follow a four step model and gather the tools for spring boarding the S-Curve. The four steps are:

1. Create or acquire an innovation lab.

2. Translate the insights into a value proposition and a pivot plan.

3. Create the supply chain trigger plan.

4. Create a business process engineering plan.

CREATE OR PROCURE AN INNOVATION LAB

In the business model, shown in Figure 10.1, the customer operations for P&G has developed a new trial tool for understanding the direct to customer sales through the Tide club. Customers can subscribe to a regular shipment of Tide detergent delivered to their door step. While this is a new business stream and may offer some cost savings by skipping the wholesales and retailer, the main thrust of the program is to understand the customer willingness to get products delivered direct. This adds valuable insights to the customer behavior and their competitive shopping habits. Unilever's Dollar Shave Club is a similar initiative.

One of the key activities that I engage in, when working with a new team, is an exercise on customer priorities. Too often in a large organization, the customer goals are diluted when it reaches the operating level. For example, at an automotive OEM, the following is an exercise that I undertake with the team. Each workshop participant will present a story of a customer, who has recently purchased our automobile or has considered our automobile and purchased a competition. It is called a story of "I am". An example of one such story is in Figure 10.3.

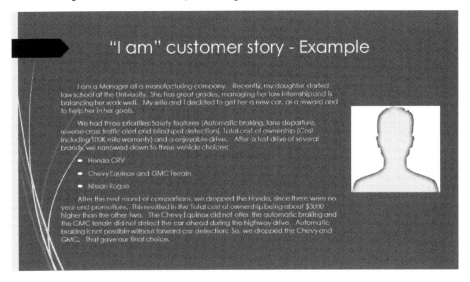

Figure 10.3: "I am" customer workshop

The idea is not to create a new mechanism for customer insight, but to create a culture of readiness for customer inputs. In many engineering organizations, the operating divisions are so far removed from the actual day to day customer needs and wants that the end customer is no longer the prime focus of the business.

TRANSLATE THE INSIGHT INTO A VALUE PROPOSITION

Successful companies have created in-house hackathons or innovation labs to solve customer problems. By recognizing the power of group thought and creativity any problem can be tackled in multiple ways. While Google X labs and Microsoft labs are the well-known companies with innovation labs, other companies such as Parker Hannifin with robotic exoskeleton for paraplegic mobility and Sephora with Color IQ, the computer based color matching for makeup, are excellent examples of successful innovation projects. The QFD/CIPD tool introduced in chapter 4, is used extensively when new tech is a key ingredient for the innovation.

Rule #12 (Inspired by Steve Jobs)	Before tech, customer experience is the first check, Tech first, then customer, will break your neck.

An quick integration is to eliminate the middleman and take your products directly to the market. But this means the training of company personnel to take on the additional responsibility for retail duties and this is never a quick fix.

One of the lessons of the innovation lab at Parker is the "production-ization" or the fast pivot to get the product into the market in a short window. This requires the company to springboard the current products and launch new products very quickly. Timeline for such changes is laid out day by day for a quick pivot.

TRIGGER POINTS FOR SUPPLY CHAIN

The change point for an organization is the identification of the new product and the supply chain requirements for the launch of the new product or service. The new launch may be the same product launched for a different segment or through a different channel for a new value proposition. Zara, the clothing retailer has executed this strategy well.

"Zara may look like fashion, but the real insight is how it achieves four times more profitability than most apparel retailers. Zara's performance is more than higher turn and margin; its model reduces inventory risk in a highly uncertain business." - Sourcing Journal Guest Editorial (The Zara Gap – And Retail Denial, 2015). For more about Zara, please read the enclosed sidebar.

Zara and Sourcing Innovation

Zara, the clothing store, founded by Amancia Ortega, is a sourcing innovation leader. The Company has shaken up the clothing retail industry with innovative supply chain and is one of the fastest growing fashion clothing retail.

In the normal fashion business, the fall fashions are debuted on a catwalk in spring. The successful designs are then sourced and manufactured in the supply chains and arrive in time for the first day of fall, with a minimum timeline of 6 months from the first fashion catwalk to the first day of season sale. Gap, H&M, Uniqlo, Topshop and others follow this trend.

However, the products have an uncertain demand when the season starts. A retail estimate is that about 20% of the products will be sold at a discount, while another 20% of the products will be sold out in half the season.

So, Zara has a new supply chain plan for matching supply and demand. Zara has brilliantly reduced the length of the chain, many times doing a vertical integration with the acquisition of the manufacturing unit and has saved a minimum of 90 days in the fashion arrival by using local sources for the manufacturing.

 Continued	This way, the retailer can keep a continuous feed of supply into the store during the season with no stock outs or huge discounts, unlike the other retailers. In the world of fashion, where Abercrombie & Fitch, Gap and others are cutting down the number of stores, Zara is in a growth spurt with plans to open many new locations over the next year, including expanding in competitive locations of Asia. Zara has focused on "fast fashion" where upstream supply chain flexibility is tied to downstream product profitability. Zara's **strategic network design** incorporates the **decoupling inventory** planning for the fast changes required in the new business model.

Rule #13	Other factors being constant, the longer the chain, higher the risk.

Many times, there is a conflict between the plant efficiency and the supply chain efficiency. Plant efficiency is measured in labor hours per units produced. However, in supply chain efficiency, I always recommend that the plant efficiency be measured in labor hours worked in a time-period per units sold in the same time-period. This puts into focus that the manpower utilization at the plant, should not be an independent metric, but be tied to the productivity of the business as-a-whole, rather than just the plant. Transparency and **data visibility** are key metrics in the plant and in the supply chain.

Rule #14	Supply chain full efficiency can happen only through chain transparency

In the Just-in-time practices developed by Toyota, there is a clear link in efficiency practices and the supply chain data visibility. This works for all practices of supply chain, not just in Just-in-time. Toyota, around the world, has pioneered Just-in-time, a form of supply chain visibility in the supply chain, where the suppliers see the production demand on a real time. The operational efficiency can be achieved only through supply chain transparency and single point demand forecasting.

Rule #15	The start point for any supply chain is accurate and accountable demand forecasting.

MANAGE BUSINESS PROCESS REENGINEERING

Business process change is one of the most complicated tasks in the organization. Given the organizational vision and purpose, the nature of organization continues along as a steady ship, with vision as a rudder. Since business needs change regularly, the vision must change to guide the organization through the required changes to be effective in the new environment. In small organizations, the unfreeze-change-refreeze model, proposed by Lewin, works well.

For instance, in a large gas station chain such as Quick Trip (QT), the day to day working of the store is controlled by the corporate policies established by QT headquarters, in Nashville, TN. However, change is possible when the "corporate trainer" will regularly visit and review the working of the team. The trainer may experiment with some of the policies, during the visit, offering some new product promotions and work policies to make the store more effective. There is experimentation at the store level during the visit. The policies are then frozen on his/her departure from the store. The store manager has some limited flexibility with manpower management, but not on the product availability and other business returns activities. This managed change offers a delicate balance to drive in change and works well in small operational teams (less than 50) and during the ownership change in small businesses.

Since every change is a delicate and stressful act for the team, a vision clarity should be there before the change is undertaken. All changes, big or small, need the prerequisites for the change as identified by the popular change model acronym – ADKAR in literature. ADKAR emphasizes a continuous change in small increments to get to the large goal of the organizational change.

ADKAR - Change model

Awareness for the change needed.
Desire, why the change is needed.
Knowledge, the understanding of the strategic vision.
Ability, to make the change happen.
Reinforcement, the need for constant push & monitoring.W

The most effective change mechanism for the large organization is the 7S metric. Take for instance, the multiyear supply chain goal undertaken by Dell to convert the MTO model of low inventory and high value computers into several different business streams aimed at the different needs of the target customers. This was a multiyear project with the multiple cycle, while the ongoing business cannot be compromised but the long-term goal of multiple business streams was realized. Such a big company change requires a framework for the execution. The McKinsey 7S framework is ideal for this scenario. The 7 "S" are:

McKinsey 7S

Structure: A structural analysis, how the structure should be during, and after the change.

System: Identify and evaluate the existing systems and the new pieces that need to be installed and updated.

Skills: The change will not work without the right skills for the new systems.

Style: The style is the culture of the business, which should be addressed during the changes.

Staff: The people and their strengths of diversity.

Strategy: The competitive strategy for successful future of the business.

Shared values: Understanding of the common values.

This 7S framework helps the self-reflection and management insight and drives the change forward.

The supply chain change model at Dell

Dell has undergone a multiyear supply chain change to transform the business from a CTO (Configure To Order) retail business to multiple streams that satisfy retail and corporate customers. Before this journey, Dell created a vision of identifying the voice of the customer and transforming the company into individual streams.

The voice of the customer planning is shown below in Figure 10.5. The multiyear supply chain plan was orchestrated through an innovation leader (and an innovation lab). Now Dell offers differentiated products to different segments in a journey from 2008 to now.

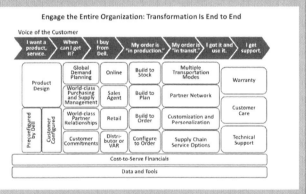

Figure 10.5 Voice of the Customer plan

(Source Dell)

Many companies use the portfolio approach for this supply chain segmentation. Dell had a well-established supply chain for custom orders. Now, with the growth of Dell's business customers, it has created the same style of segmented supply chain. Same components may be procured from two different sources, or on two different time schedules.

Each stream will have a unique cost, the cost to serve, and the customer will be charged this unique cost based on his service timing and other requirements. Thus, Dell maintains its segmented supply base to accommodate retail customer orders as custom order, while it maintains a small stock for corporate customers that are MTS (made to stock). By keeping the two streams separate, Dell has a low inventory cost and is the most profitable computer manufacturer for that volume.

Disruption changes are equally likely in large companies as they are in small and medium companies. This chapter covered the tasks for the continuous innovation process, especially in large companies and their supply chain enablers for this transformation.

***

CHAPTER 11
PURPOSE DRIVEN COMPANY

"It's a paradox that companies are more profitable when they focus more on purpose instead of profits."

–BBC Capital on the HBR Business case for purpose.

In a book of business and supply chain strategies, it might be odd to find a business model that is based on a purpose other than profits. But just as said in the BBC Capital quote above, this business strategy is a paradoxical contradiction. With a higher purpose ranging from the greater social good to a green sustainable business, this business model is an add-on and is very versatile. So, please stay with me till the end of chapter, so that we can review the full picture.

Companies are fueled by profits. But some companies have modified their core business plan and created a new one, based on a purpose driven softer game plan. Take for instance, the company, Honest Tea. The company was founded by Seth Goldman and his college professor, Barry Nablebuff. Seth's intent was to bring an organic tea in the market, that was natural in taste and not heavily sweetened. In addition, Honest Tea's game plan was to establish fair trade dealing with its suppliers. From its humble startup beginnings in 1998, the company rose to annual sales of 1.5 million cases in 7 years. In a crowded market place with several me-too products, Coca Cola spotted Honest Tea and acquired a minority stake for $43 million in 2011.

The brand-attractiveness of the purpose driven companies in the marketplace is easily visible. Nike, the brand ranked 17th globally by Interbrand[8], uses ocean skimmed plastic in its products and recycles old shoes by grinding, while Toyota, ranked 7th globally, has established carbon neutral plants around the world, all with a purpose driven mindset. In

---

[8] https://www.interbrand.com/best-brands/best-global-brands/2018/ranking/

some cases, large multinationals have made significant drive for the socially minded stakeholders, with Clorox acquiring Burt's Bees and Unilever acquiring Ben & Jerry.

The resonance effect works within the company as well. Statistics say that 71% of the millennials in the general workforce are disconnected. In stark contrast, a recent HBR case reports that 84% of the employees in a purpose driven company are engaged. With most customers willing to switch to a purpose driven brand, if cost and quality are equal, the purpose driven company has a promising profit outlook. Research has shown that each employee in a purpose driven company becomes a **brand ambassador**, creating a "rowing together effect", which makes the company 12x more than the average company (Keller, 2015).

Rule #16 (Ms. Ha Nguyen, Omidyar Network)	Passion is about finding yourself. Purpose is about losing yourself – in something bigger than yourself.

So how do you find your purpose? Many startups have a higher purpose in their DNA. LendUp is one such company that markets a "LendUp Ladder". This product enables low income and customers with poor credit to get out of continuously refinancing payday loans and into financial health step-by-step.

Many others discover their purpose during crisis. DTE, the Detroit Energy utility was one such entity. When the great recession hit Detroit in 2008, the company performance was in shambles. DTE was facing massive layoffs to meet its budget. The morale was low and an internal Gallup poll score on employee engagement showed the numbers were at rock bottom. Gerry Anderson, the new CEO, tried several training programs but with no success. In 2008, he decided to take on the employee commitment requirement to the employees and the union. As the first step, he made a promise with the employees that if the financial health can be improved with greater participation, then he would commit to reduce or avoid layoffs. Teams worked hand in hand to re-scope existing and committed projects so that the performance measures can be achieved at a fraction of the cost.

For example, instead of getting new digital controls for the plant, the team identified that the old circuit boards could be replaced for a fraction of the cost.

Secondly, the company would drive for a higher purpose, to be "a force for prosperity in the Southeast Michigan area and to the State". In the months that followed, DTE employees were the leaders in local civic organizations, such as Habitat for Humanity, United Way and Literacy improvements for immigrants. DTE and the area improved together over time. The results speak for themselves. Over a period of 10 years, DTE showed a 275% improvement in shareholder value, three times the achievement by its peer average.

In startup circles, it is well known that companies with a higher purpose have a significant edge over others. The rule below is a common driver in startups.

Rule #17 (Startup rule)	Startups grow through a higher mission.

Now let's look at another common mission with many companies.

IS GREEN YOUR PURPOSE?

Imagine, the world in 2050. You wake up in the morning after a good night of sleep. It is winter and snowy outside, but the house is set to a balmy 70° F. You know that the underground pipes heating the house use a community wide geothermal energy plant and require low maintenance. Your diet is sustainably farmed fish. The major news that morning is that the shipping companies have retired the last oil-fired ship, now every ship in the ocean is driven by sustainable new energy sources. The world is now using 80% less oil than in the 2020s. Your clothes and lifestyles are environmentally friendly. You travel on autonomous hydrogen powered vehicles that emit water vapor, instead of greenhouse gases.

This scene might as well have been from the book, "The World We Made," by environmentalist, Sir Jonathon Porritt. While, you may or may not agree with Jonathon on his hope and alarm in the futuristic world, it is clear to see the necessity and more & more companies today are moving towards sustainable and environmentally friendly operation. The triple bottom line for these companies is the financial gain, combined with environmental excellence and social betterment. Improved efficiency in reducing environmental waste can provide a financial incentive, as well an enormous goodwill for the product and the brand image of the company.

Many industries that consume high amount of resources, such as chemicals, electronics, automotive and heavy engineering have made giant strides in environmental excellence. Others that are ahead of the curve, have aligned with the triple bottom line concept. Examples of the activities that fall within the triple bottom line include:

- Reduced and effective packaging and its cost savings.

- Design products for reuse and recycling.

- Reduce the environmental effect of product and processes from Life Cycle Analysis.

- Reverse logistics to reacquire recycle-able customer return materials.

- Better quality and shorter lead-times due to ISO 14000 implementation for disassembly and re-use of products over their usage lifetime.

- Green manufacturing, where the plant is carbon neutral by efficient processing or compensatory processing.

- Safer work areas and warehousing.

- Improved safety and lower health costs.

- Reduced labor, lower recruitment and reduced turnover due to better working conditions.

- Higher motivation and less absenteeism at work from better working conditions.

The first step for the company for the green supply chain, is to establish the Executive Champion within the company. Noel Kinder is the Chief Sustainability Officer at Nike, and his motto, "At Nike, we know that the future of sport is interlocked with the future of our planet. That understanding serves as our North Star for sustainability." Nike's business model is shown in Figure 11.1.

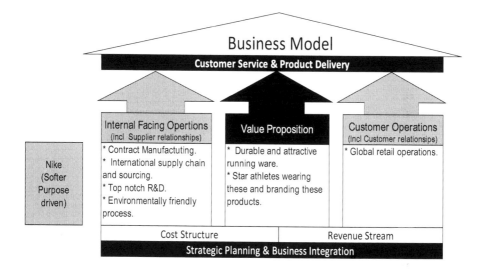

Figure 11.1: The Purpose driven model for Nike

In India, water is a scarce commodity, since most of the mountain streams terminate in the North, while the South is largely dependent on monsoon rains. So, a key initiative in India for many businesses is to harvest, store and irrigate the corporate building gardens with rain water. Mahindra Lifespaces, a real estate developer, is a part of a large multinational conglomerate, with a market cap of US$ 19 billion. It operates a 1500-acre industrial city in Chennai, India, were the bath water from the homes is recycled for plant irrigation and the company follows a zero-landfill waste policy. This is done through managing waste at every level - from prevention to minimization, to reuse, recycling, energy recovery and disposal. Plastic bags are banned in grocery stores. The buses and street lights are operated by converting organic waste into CNG. The trash cans are solar powered for garbage compaction and are IoT enabled, managing the pickup when full, while optimizing the garbage truck route. Obviously, being named as the

#1 Green city in India, has its marketing advantages. It now houses 150+ Companies and their 40000+ employees.

Green is a purpose that requires a well-planned supply chain. Enclosed is the supply chain strategy for the green supply chain (Figure 11.2).

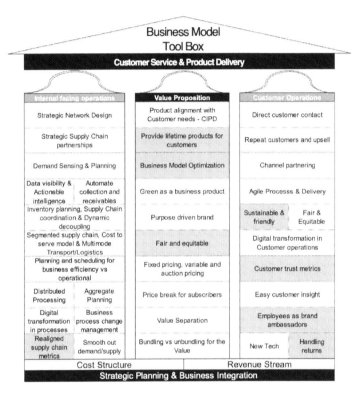

Figure 11.2: The SMART tool box for Higher purpose Co.

FROM A LINEAR TO A CIRCULAR ECONOMY

Some companies have gone past the green supply chain and the linear economy. In a linear economy, the product or service offered follows the "take-make-dispose" process, generating substantial waste at the end of life. On the other hand, if the cradle to grave product planning was refocused into a cradle to cradle, where the product end of life materials is recycled into new products, then we have a circular economy. ***Handling returns*** and ***reverse logistics*** is a crucial strategy for circular economy companies.

In companies with a circular economy purpose, recycling, reuse, resource reduction and reverse logistics are the way of life. Examples of companies range from Mohawk Flooring Co that recycles carpet materials to Johnson Controls that has a 99% recyclable battery.

Inyenyeri is a Rwandan Social enterprise company started by Eric Reynolds, a California native who is trying to improve the lives of locals with a for-profit enterprise. Inyenyeri distributes a low smoke emitting wood stove that is several generations better than the stick burning or charcoal burning stoves that are popular in Rwanda. In the fast urbanizing cities in Rwanda, the wood pellets that Inyenyeri sells are 30 to 40% cheaper than charcoal, and in rural Rwanda, the poor can freely exchange fewer wood sticks for the more efficient wood pellets. This saves the drudgery in the villagers foraging for wood sticks, needing two or three bundles of wood sticks per day to keep the cooking fires on. The lack of water vapor in the chips gives little or no smoke, enabling the villagers to have a healthier life.

Inyenyeri is "on the verge of freeing much of humanity from the deadly scourge of the cooking fire, and toxic smoke, that is causing lung disease, cataracts etc. By better efficiency and no toxic smoke, to save the forest cover and help rescue the planet from the wrath of climate change," according to Eric. Such enterprises are supported by the UN sustainability initiative.

Study of the employees of such companies, shows that each person is typically committed to the company in work and in purpose. These companies flourish from the synergy with ***employees being the brand ambassadors***.

***

PART 3

WHERE DO YOU
GO
FROM HERE?

CHAPTER 12

SUPPLY CHAIN MATURITY

	The yardstick measure of a supply chain execution is "the perfect order".	
	The Perfect order is defined as orders delivered	
Rule #18 (Adapted from Ariba Live)	to the	RIGHT PLACE,
	with the	RIGHT PRODUCT,
	at the	RIGHT TIME,
	in the	RIGHT CONDITION,
	in the	RIGHT PACKAGE,
	in the	RIGHT QUANTITY,
	with the	RIGHT DOCUMENTATION,
	to the	RIGHT CUSTOMER,
	with the	CORRECT INVOICE.

A required KPI for supply chain is the problem solving measure, if and why a perfect order is not met.

As you can see from the previous chapters, supply chain is a competitive advantage and a key ingredient in the business strategy transformation of successful companies. It is the authors' conviction that companies should layout their supply chain strategy as a part of their business plan and this may range from lean implementation to multi-segmented or any of the several other strategies discussed earlier and found in today's leading disruptive businesses. Thoughtful execution of each of these strategies in alignment with business planning, creates a strong brand for the company. From the examples in prior chapters, it is clear that many companies have customized their supply chain strategy and created this competitive advantage, positioning themselves in a strategic lead.

In general, each company should have a mature supply chain process and should be ready for competitive challenges that are ever present in today's marketplace. Business leaders grapple with this maturity every day but in our reviews, we found many supply chains are reactive rather than strategic or proactive in their outlook. So, in this chapter we will discuss the maturity model for supply chains.

A maturity model is a structured framework for assisting companies in their continuous improvement process to reach a better state of competitive readiness. The model provides a means for each situation to be analyzed from multiple variables in three dimensions. Each variable in turn provides an opportunity to improve the agility of the company. Enclosed is the maturity model that the authors have successfully executed in developing companies in the automotive supplier base, hospitality and the small business arena. With minimal additional work, the model can be used in a wider range of industry applications.

The maturity model framework contains four levels, three dimensions and twelve variables. A company's commitment is measured across these three dimensions: the process rigor, the working culture and the investment commitment. The supply chain maturity of each company can be at one of four levels. Level 0 is the reactive supply chain that is common in many companies. Issues are escalated based on the urgency of need and constant firefighting mode is used to drive issues to closure. The most mature level is the dynamic supply chain and requires planning and reorganization in the supply chain process and networks, for the level upgrade to achieve this maturity. It also requires business alignment with the necessary resource deployment. Figure 12.1 shows the four levels of supply chain maturity.

	Supply Chain Maturity
Level 0	Reactive supply chain
Level 1	Integrative supply chain (with buffer planning)
Level 2	Strategic & Collaborative supply chain
Level 3	Dynamic & Proactive supply chain

Figure 12.1: Supply Chain Maturity Levels

Supply Chain Maturity Dimensions & Variables

Process Rigor
1. Customer Service Management
2. Strategic Planning
3. S & Op planning (Supply Chain and Operations)
4. Process drive
5. Innovation drive
6. Clear Organizational roles
7. Demand planning

Relationship Culture
1. Work Culture
2. Supplier Relationship
3. Aligned KPIs

Investment Commitment and ROI
1. Process and IT investment
2. Electronic Commerce Commitment

Figure 12.2: Supply Chain Maturity Dimensions

The supply chain maturity variables are used for audit and planning for maturity upgrades. The three dimensions and its associated variables are shown in Figure 12.2.

THE REACTIVE SUPPLY CHAIN

As we had identified earlier, the most commonly seen supply chain status for the companies is the Reactive supply chain. The process rigor is the most common missing piece in these companies. Customer service, in such a company is handled on a case by case basis. The owner or the CEO typically does the strategic planning. It is done irregularly and is very fragmented. The planning process is not laid out and cannot be called a business process. Typically, these companies are centered around a product or marketable service, that is their reason for existence. Strategic planning process is informal and ad hoc. S & Op meetings do not occur regularly and when they occur, are used for firefighting to solve the pressing issue at hand. The general motto for supply chain may well be that the squeaky wheel gets the oil. Demand forecast is based on a gut feel or a historical plan rather than a demand planning. Improvements are not planned and the future product innovation and associated resource planning may not be structured.

Most often, level 0 companies are in general retail or in hospitality. In this industry, the level 0 work culture is not productive but may not hinder the day to day operations, due to the small operation base. However, even in these industries, at the time of business sale, a poor culture will cause unnecessary damage to the business value.

At level 0, the work culture may be purely confrontational, rather than collaborative between the employees and the management. The organizational structure is also not very effective. Problems are assigned by the business leader to task owners. Supplier relationships are not very clear. Frequently, the business may switch suppliers based on cost or any other one parameter, such as a one-time delay, sales person interaction, etc. Level 0 is not very effective in medium or large businesses but may work in the small business operations, if the leader can manage the detail. A large gas station chain was having frequent power interruptions in Brighton, Michigan, during the winter of 2007. Calls to the local utility company did not yield any quick fixes. Since the gas station was a part of larger company, with several gas stations along I-96, we were able to get the utility company to make appropriate changes with the collective bargaining power of the gas station chain.

This is common in level 0 supply chain. The individual business units interact with each supplier, and loose the collaborative benefit of the group.

Organizations grow and mature with the right investment at the right time for the business. IT capabilities and Electronic commerce have invaded every business and even small businesses are not immune to the need to invest to grow the business.

A level 1 automotive supply chain firm in Italy, made some rapid changes during a time of economic downturn. The company closed its production line in Italy & Southern Germany, moved the line to a low cost country and oursourced key components to new suppliers in the new region. Unfortunately, the new suppliers for high pressure rubber hoses and rubber boots, did not have the right formulation of rubber, and this key knowledge did not transfer during the outsouring. The new rubber formulation from the low cost country supplier, had a oil content that mixed with the operating fluid and caused contamination failures. So the sourcing decision had to reversed until the local supply development was reworked, with a one year delay to product launch.

Such strategic concerns are the key differentiators for the level 1 and level 2 companies, and the need to improve to level 3.

THE INTEGRATIVE & COLLABORATIVE SUPPLY CHAINS

Many times, the businesses see the need to manage the inventory in the supply chain. So, the Level 1 operation, focusses on inventory smoothing. The bull whip effect, discussed in chapter 4, is a key focus, since such an affect wreaks havoc in the supply chain, with huge disruptions in product availability. Several other processes are aligned to the buffer planning and the location of this buffer.

Level 1 organizations treat all customers the same and customer service is a one-size-fits-all plan. Level 2 is the collaborative supply chain, where the strategic customers have a separate customer service. R&D is the driver for the new products and the workplace culture is based on the employee management consultation rather than strictly hierarchical.

A level 1 automotive supply chain firm in Italy, made some rapid changes during a time of economic downturn. The company closed its production line in Italy & Southern Germany, moved the line to a low cost country and outsourced key components to new suppliers in the new region. Unfortunately, the new suppliers for high pressure rubber hoses and rubber boots, did not have the right formulation of rubber, and this key knowledge did not transfer during the outsouring. The new rubber formulation from the low cost country supplier, had a oil content that mixed with the operating fluid and caused contamination failures. So the sourcing decision had to reversed until the local supply development was reworked, with a one year delay to product launch.

Such strategic concerns are the key differentiators for the level 1 and level 2 companies, and the need to improve to level 3.

THE DYNAMIC SUPPLY CHAIN

For many companies, a dynamic supply chain is an aspirational model. Here the customer service is segmented, just as the supply chain and the product delivery may be segmented as well. In this way, each customer can pay for the right level of service and get the service he or she deserves. At Amazon, Prime customers may have guaranteed delivery dates for their products, while ordinary customer must pay extra for each shipment, wait for the consolidation of goods into fewer shipments or receive the shipment on a regular slower shipment time. In some online services, it is possible to customize your service level beyond shipping options and pay after the choice.

Integrating strategic planning is also a key element of the dynamic supply chain. Supply chain planning drives competitive positioning of innovation and future products using cross functional teams. The strategic planning cross functional team is bringing results at Apple. Recent company reports have identified that Apple is planning to migrate from hardware leadership to leading content delivery. In the near term, Apple & Android are nearing the hardware life cycle innovation limits with the current technology and AI and other software, content is the next frontier.

S & Op process is now a structured process in the dynamic supply chain. The planning window is a rolling period and at the end of each period, the rollover is seamless. Synchronization of vertical and horizontal S & Op is mandated across business segments. There is a 5-year advanced plan for plant layout & capacity and a 2-year execution plan. A S & Op dashboard is visible to the business leaders with a single forecast across all business units. The forecasting will have drill down capability up to the SKU level and is a part of the overall planning process.

The Dynamic supply chain company is process driven with a continuous improvement DNA. In the automotive supplier base, if the first project is executed in 24-months, subsequent projects are expected to meet percentage improved delivery targets and/or improved timing. This is especially true with vehicle and powertrain new product launches. A lessons-learned process recaps the end of the project and starts the next one. Projects are aligned across businesses with the business results being outcome driven. Each team member is rated on a balanced and cross functional scorecard, which is integrated horizontally and vertically across the business, with cost and service metric.

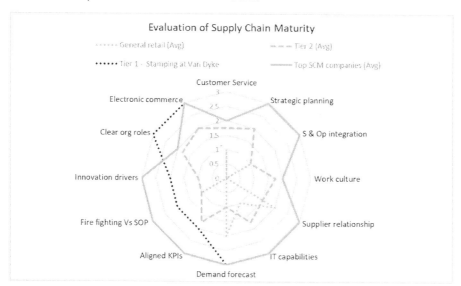

Figure 12.3: Evaluation of Supply Chain Maturity across many suppliers.

A comparative evaluation of several businesses along the maturity growth path is shown in Figure 12.3. The Tier 1 Stamping Company, run by Happy Singh, discussed in Chapter 9, is shown in the evaluation as well.

Figure 12.4: Supplier Selection process for an OE Ecosystem

Some OEs have taken the maturity and the evaluation further. One OE has used the metrics from the supplier evaluation in selecting the supply base for its flagship product.

Based on the self-evaluation of the suppliers, the OE rates the suppliers in two categories. One of the factors is the Management resolve, which measures the commitment of the management team to deliver the product on delivery, cost, quality and time. Management resolve is the sum of process rigor and work culture. The second metric is the investment appetite, since the returns from the business is based on the timely investment in the business. Eighteen companies were rated on these two scales. The upper right-hand quadrant representing the companies with the high management resolve and the willingness to invest to grow the business were the two key metrics and 5 suppliers in that category were invited to participate in the Ecosystem being setup for new core products. This is shown in Figure 12.4.

In summary, supply chain strategy and the supply chain maturity are key drivers in the business transformation strategy. Companies can leverage these strengths as springboards for the next launch or to reorganize the business around the new business model.

***

CHAPTER 13

THE FUTURE OF SUPPLY CHAIN

Most companies struggle with business tweaks and incremental change. These tweaks are common during down cycle, but they create operational gaps that must be managed. However, these tweaks typically reduce the competitiveness and don't contribute to the long term business growth strategy.

At the meeting in 2002 from Chapter 1, Joe and I (Shawn) discussed this issue and identified the need for a specific business process to evaluate the necessity for change. In this business process, the first task was to isolate the business drivers that demand the change. Since supply chain processes represent a substantial value of the company, the business transition strategy requires reframing the supply chain structure in terms of the customer value proposition. Also, during this process, the evolving new rules of competition creates the need for new capabilities within the organization. These capabilities should be planned before the transition.

BUSINESS TRANSITION WORKSHOP

Our business change process recommends a regular business strategy workshop. The key members of the business, "the business strategy board" should meet quarterly to assess the business needs and to evaluate the business model for the future. For instance, in the small business enterprise of a retail service station, the owner was traditionally responsible for identifying the product mix - the fast or slow moving items, developing a retail pricing scale, stocking his store and the P&L. So, through a business transition workshop, we recommended that this job be now outsourced to the wholesaler, who brought in the product variety to the retail establishment, recommended prices, marked the correct price per the owner's instructions and managed the restocking of items.

This gave the owner more time to run the business and identify customer trends. Similarly, in the stamping facility in Chapter 3, the logistics firm added value by bringing in the raw stock at the right time. So, supply chain intelligence was created.

The dynamic supply chain introduced in Chapter 12 creates a business focus for the supply chain in the company. This maturity in supply chain elevates the contribution from a functional role to a process for the company's success. The supply chain gets segmented based on the customer needs and the end-result is a targeted benefit and improved margin for the company. A dynamic supply chain provides additional opportunities of revenue for the company. Strategic planning and continuous improvement become the DNA of the company performance.

Supply chain is no longer measured within the confines of functional performance, but on a balanced scorecard for company wide contribution. Managing supply chain complexity is a key element for productive results. Too many segments can cause unnecessary strain on the results compilation. Each change should be evaluated for its return of investment.

SUPPLY CHAIN TECHNOLOGY MEGATRENDS

The megatrends in supply chain will dictate the future path of supply chain. As expensive tasks are automated and become common, new modes of business will evolve.

The supply chain team should evaluate each trend and its applicability on a routine basis. Some of these trends are.

1. **Robotic Automation:** Supply Chain operations for companies are incorporating Robotic Process Automation (RPA), where the organization can deploy smart application bots that will take common operational tasks and automate them, improving uptime and accuracy. Administrative tasks such as order taking, ordering and managing inventory levels can now be performed automatically.

In the future, response to quotes and automating of routine processes can improve efficiency, reduce waste and reduce cost. Also process scale up required for the newer business models can be easily executed without the need for new hires and training. The automated process can manage supply contracts, vendor relations and other simpler supply chain processes as well. The CIO magazine estimates that 80% of the business process outsourcing work will be eliminated by RPA. (Bendor-Samuel, 2018).

2. **3D Printing brings local manufacturing:** In the On-demand economy, product delivery expectations have gone from waiting periods to instant delivery. Alibaba and Amazon have established extensive supply chains and delivery mechanisms to enable same day and same hour deliveries. Other companies are turning to 3D printing to create products, subassemblies & components to speed up their product creation timeline. The cost of shipment from a far away supplier can be reduced by on demand printing, reducing work in process inventory and shipping risks. During a demonstration at the Center of manufacturing innovation in Knoxville, Tennessee, a 1940s style Willis Jeep was manufactured with 3D components and assembled on site. 3D printing creates a true on-demand process so that the manufacturing can become local. It may be possible in the not to distant future, for companies to sell their designs to the end customers. Customers can receive the 3D source file through email, and then "manufacture" them at their home for their own use, using 3D printing.

3. **The Last mile delivery:** Another innovation driving supply chain is the ability to deliver products to the end customers in time. While the task of getting the product to the end customer's city can be done well with today's network, the delivery of the product to the customer's final address, is the most expensive and inefficient and requires a custom solution. Amazon and some others are experimenting with drone delivery. Drone will improve road

congestion but require some air flight regulation. 3D Robotics, the drone software company, reports that the current drone software is extremely easy to use, and user can easily create a flight path. It is estimated that the construction companies can reduce their cost and timing substantially during site inspections by using drones. (Mansour, 2018)

4. **IoT and Sensors Everywhere:** IoT is a widely used term for sensors with their data and controls accessible over the internet. Many of these sensors may include GPS tracking. With the sensor cost coming down, IoT will have a universal effect in every industry. Today industries such as self driving cars, to automatic on-demand irrigation in farming have IoT sensors in the field. The most common IoT sensor in supply chain, is the RFID and similar technologies that allow the automatic ID of shipping goods, even across borders with automated document verification for customs. IoT can provide asset tracking, inventory tracking, connected fleets and accuracy of operations.

5. **Distributed Security:** Blockchain is another growing application, that provides secure connected blocks for identifying the history of an entity. Block chains are being used for verifying the origin and authenticity of goods manufactured.

6. **Machine Learnings and Automation:** Machine learning and AI is the field of study where the computer pattern recognition identifies common sequences in operations and automates them. An early example is Google, where Gmail will provide reply suggestions to your emails, based on word patterns in the mail. Advanced machine learnings help detect obstacles for self driving cars and automatic GPS routing around accidents.

PLANNING THE TRANSITION

The business transition strategy is one of the key outputs of the SMART supply chain. The long road to changeover, has some low hanging fruits for immediate benefit, while the business transition strategy typically takes about 6 months for small businesses and 12 to 24 months for fortune 500 size companies. The road to changeover, starts with the business SWOT, identifying the strengths, weaknesses, opportunities and threats in the current business climate. The realities are clearly pinpointed by the business drivers.

Each business model and its supply chain strategy offer unique advantages that can be targeted for your business.

***

LIST OF BUSINESS CASES IN PART 1

- Adient plc (Johnson Controls Seating)

- AirBnb.com

- Amazon

- Apple

- Barnes & Noble Vs Borders

- Kmart Vs Target & Walmart

- IBM

- LinkedIn

- Parker Hannifin Corporation

- Tier 1 Stamping Company, Sterling Heights, MI

- Troy Restaurants LLC, Troy, MI

- TVS Scooters

LIST OF BUSINESS CASES IN PART 2

- 7-11 Franchise

- Alibaba Tmall and Taobao

- Apple iPhone

- Apple iTunes

- Dell Computers

- DTE Energy, Detroit, MI

- Hilti Tools

- Honest Tea

- Kalamazoo Hotels, Kalamazoo, MI

- Lansing Storage Companies, Lansing, MI

- Mr. B's bar and grill, Detroit Area, MI

- Munro Gas Station, Munro, MI

- Netflix

- Nike Co.

- Proctor & Gamble Vs Unilever

- Quick Trip Gas Stations, Nashville, TN

- Rolls Royce Engines

- Shanghai GM, Shanghai, China

- Sony Play station Vs Microsoft Xbox

- Suzuki & Maruti Suzuki, India

- Telsa Vs Gm & Ford

- Tier 1 Stamping Company, Sterling Heights

- Ypsilanti Towing Co, Ypsilanti, MI

- ZARA

LIST OF BUSINESS CASES IN PART 3

- Retail convenience stores, Toledo, OH

- Tier 1 Automotive supplier, Germany

- Valero Gas stations, Brighton, MI

REFERENCES

Keller, Valerie (2015). A Business case for purpose, A Harvard Business Review Analytic Services Report, hbr.org/hbr-analytic-services, Downloaded: Nov 15, 2018.

Srivastava, S. (2007). Green supply-chain management: A state-of-the-art literature review. International Journal of Management Reviews, 9(1), 53-80. https://onlinelibrary.wiley.com/doi/abs/10.1111/j.1468-2370.2007.00202.x, Downloaded: Dec 10, 2017.

Arena, U., Mastellone, M., & Perugini, F. (2003). Life cycle assessment of a plastic packaging recycling system. International 1 Journal of Life Cycle Assessment, 8, 92–98. https://link.springer.com/article/10.1007%2FBF02978432. Downloaded: Jan 15, 2017

SJ Guest editorial (March 12, 2015), The Zara Gap – And Retail Denial, Sourcing Journal, https://sourcingjournal.com/topics/retail/zara-gap-retail-denial-thorbeck-25370/, downloaded 24 Nov 2018

Claire Beale (2016), Disrupting the disruptors: how Unilever plans to rock the boat, July 28, 2016, https://www.campaignlive.co.uk/article/disrupting-disruptors-unilever-plans-rock-boat/1403746, Downloaded: Oct 12, 2017

Stephen J Lubben (2011), A short timeline in Borders bankruptcy, New York times, February 16, 2011, https://dealbook.nytimes.com/2011/02/16/the-short-timeline-in-the-borders-bankruptcy/

Ahrens, N. (2013), China's competitiveness, Myth, reality and lessons for United States and Japan, Center for Strategic and International Studies, 1800 K Street, NW, Washington, DC, page 3

Bhattacharya, S. Mukhopadhyay, D., Giri, S and Katra (2014), Supply Chain Management in Indian Automotive Industry: Complexities

Challenges and Way Ahead. International Journal of Managing Value and Supply Chains (IJMVSC) Vol.5, No. 2, June 2014

Ecola, L., Rohr, C., Zmud, J., Kuhnimhof, T. and Phleps, P. (2014), The Future of Driving in Developing Countries, Institute for Mobility Research and Rand Corporation, Rand Corporation, USA, ISBN: 978-0-8330-8604-4

Shah, J. (2016), Supply Chain Management, Text and Cases, Pearson India Educational Services Pvt, Ltd, Chennai, India. ISBN: 978093-125-4820-6

Walter, E. & Walter, R. (2016), Data Acquisition from HD Vehicles Using J1939 CAN Bus, Society of Automotive Engineers, Detroit.

Stadtler, H & Kilger, C (2000), Supply Chain Management and Advanced Planning, Concepts, Models, Software and Case Studies, Springer-Verlag, Berlin, Heidelberg, New York.

Nakanishi, T. (2017), India and the global auto industry's transformation, A technology shift is underway, Asian Nikkei Review, https://asia.nikkei.com/Business/China-India-and-the-global-auto-industry-s-transformation, Downloaded 06 11 2018.

Bowen, S (2018), Total Value Optimization: Transforming your global supply chain into a competitive weapon, Stephen J Bowen, SJDB LLC, PO Box 271, Duxbury, MA 02331

Cote, C (2015), Vehicle heat maps at https://insideevs.com/chevrolet-volt-heat-map

Sarkar, S. (2017), Supply Chain revolution, AMACOM, American Management Association, New York, NY 10019.

Liker, J. (2004), The Toyota Way, 14 Management principles from the world's greatest manufacturer, McGraw Hill, NY

Martin, J. (2007), Lean Six Sigma for Supply Chain Management, A ten step process, McGraw Hill, New York, NY

McBride, D. (2003), The 7 Wastes in Manufacturing, https://www. emsstrategies.com/dm090203article2.html, Downloaded Oct 11 2018.

Durea, M and Strugariu, R. (2014), An Introduction to Nonlinear Optimization Theory, De Gruyter Open Ltd, Warsaw/Berlin.

Dollar, D. and Wei, S (2007), Underutilized Capital, Finance and Development, A quarterly magazine of the IMF, Website: users.nber. org/~wei/data/ underutilized_capital.pdf, Downloaded 08 11 2018.

Price Water Coopers (2008), Sourcing and logistics in China, Cost processes and strategies of German companies in the Chinese market, Price Water Coopers and Bundesverband Materialwirtschaft, Einkauf und Logistik e. V (BME), Germany.

CIO Team (2009), Maruti Suzuki Gets New Markets with a Transparent Supply Chain, http://www.cio.in/case-study/maruti-suzuki-gets-new-markets-transparent-supply-chain, Downloaded 08 11 2018

Julka, T., Jain, SS & Singh, A. (2014), Supply Chain and Logistics Management Innovations at Maruti Suzuki India Limited, International Journal of Management and Social Sciences Research (IJMSSR), Volume 3, No. 3, March 2014

Grajczyk, K. (2013), Multi-tier Supply Chain Visibility in Automotive Industry, How do automotive OEMs gain transparency and visibility into their global supply chain, Lap Lambert Academic Publishing, Saarbrucken, Deutschland.

Griffith, Erin (2017), Why do startups fail, because hardware is hard, https://www.wired.com/story/why-do-startups-fail-because-hardware-is-hard/, Wired Magazine, San Francisco, CA, USA, 9th September 2017.

Osterwalder, Alexander & Pigneur Yves (2010), Business Model Generation, John Wiley & Sons, Hoboken, NJ

Bendor-Samuel, Peter, (2018) https://www.cio.com/article/3269217/robotic-process-automation-is-reworking-supply-chains.html. Downloaded Feb 11, 2019 27.

Mansour, Steve, (2018), How drones will revolutionise the construction industry, https://www.constructionglobal.com/equipment-and-it/how-drones-will-revolutionise-construction-industry

Lin, G. et al, (2000), Extended enterprise supply chain management at IBM personal systems group and other divisions, Interfaces, Vol. 30, No 7-25

Schoenberger, C. (2002), How Kmart Blew It, Forbes Magazine, https://www.forbes.com/2002/01/18/0118kmart.html#29c1a0a15818; Downloaded Feb 5, 2017

Morgenstern, D., (2011) How will Japan earthquake affect Apple's iPad supply chain?, https://www.zdnet.com/article/how-will-japan-earthquake-affect-apples-ipad-supply-chain/

BarnesandNobles (2018) https://nook.barnesandnoble.com/u/nook-twinklelight-ereader/379004122

Hilti (2019), https://www.hilti.group/content/hilti/CP/XX/en/services/tool-services/fleet-management.html

Bailey, D. (2018), Airbnb is disruptive innovation, https://www.inc.com/dave-bailey/why-airbnb-is-disruptive-innovation-and-uber-is-not.html

Business Model Navigator (2019), Apple iPod/iTunes, https://businessmodelnavigator.com/case-firm?id=12, Downloaded on Feb 19, 2019.

Investopedia (2018) What makes Tesla business model different, https://www.investopedia.com/articles/active-trading/072115/what-makes-teslas-business-model-different.asp, Downloaded Oct 30, 2018

Nunes, P. et al (2011), Jumping the S-curve: How to Beat the Growth Cycle, Get on Top, and Stay There, Harvard Business Press, MA

Hong, Seock- Jin (2015), Is Cash-to-Cash cycle appropriate to measure supply chain performance? www.Reseachgate.net, 10.1007/978-3-319-19006-8_2

***

**For additional content, reviews
and enhanced case studies,
Please visit**

www.BusinessSmartSupplyChain.com

(Also coming soon: Study material for

APICS Certification as a Supply Chain Professional)

Printed in Great Britain
by Amazon